Blue Guitar

Rufus Goodwin

Blue Guitar

PUBLISHED BY
Market House Book Co
2208 NW Market Street, Suite 207
Seattle, Washington 98107

Library of Congress Cataloging-in-Publication Data: 2004106336

Goodwin, Rufus
Blue Guitar

ISBN 0-944638-59-7 $19.95
Printed and bound in the United States of America.
1 2 3 4 5 6 7 8 9

Cover Design: iRonanworks

Any resemblance to actual people or events, in names, traits, or details is entirely coincidental. Real names of hotels, theaters, organizations, other places, and some persons have sometimes been used where it seemed artificial not to do so, but the main characters and events in those places are fictitious. As to any errors in the customs, beliefs, facts, and interpretation of this book, they are all mine.

Contents

Part One

1   It's a Girl

achel Rosevale, the future guitarist, was born between yesterday and tomorrow. The twenty-first century might be the wrong age for her. She was either too late or too early — ahead of her time. She asked too many questions. Her first howl was a question mark. Inquisitiveness. Nothing was congenitally wrong that could be verified, and with her dark eyes, olive skin, and matted hair, she promised to be a beauty. Her features were quite round, quite regular. It was not her fault that she would be an adult after the millennium or that Israel had become an independent state in 1948. These things were beyond the reach of a baby. The theology of time is indifferent to infants — except in exceptional cases, in cases of prophets or saviors — and all Rachel's mother Deborah said was, "So, Harry, after all, it's a girl." Harry had wanted a boy, at least for the first-born.

A girl. Of course, that was the other thing wrong with Rachel.

In the crib one does not reflect on one's fate. Destiny does not come with diapers, although one is never more subject to the whims of nurture or to mercy. No human condition is more dependent, more helpless, but this did not particularly strike Rachel, who, despite all the fuss, mostly smiled.

"She smiles," said Deborah.

"Because she's a girl," said Harry.

"Maybe she knows something."

"That we don't?"

"We're not in diapers," Deborah observed.

Harry leaned back and snorted. He was good-looking still, like an Israeli fighter pilot, though he had never even been to Jerusalem. It hadn't been a question, really, not after dental school, even though Yitshak Shamir had come to Boston and held a giant rally at Brandeis. Indeed, it was impressive to have a state of one's own and one's own president. Sometimes Harry even picked up a copy of the *Jerusalem Post*, but mostly in memory of his father, old Sam. Sam had watched with rejoicing as goat by goat Israel multiplied and increased.

Sam had been a <u>real</u> Jew. His memory even went back to the fatherland, to Yiddish, the shtetls and orthodoxy of the kosher kind. The Hasidim. He had chosen America, not the Holy Land, partly because of the conflict between orthodoxy and a modern secular state. But he had not been one of those ultra-orthodox Jews who loathe the state and think Israel and Zionism are wrong, both a sin against God's will and an interference with the ways of the Redeemer, the Messiah. Sam loved the idea. A promised land to end the persecution, exile, and wandering. A promised land to give dignity and freedom to all Jews from anywhere. Never again!

Theodore Herzl, Moses Hess, Chaim Weizmann, David Ben-Gurion, and Golda Meir were all heroes to him. Every kibbutz was the outpost of a dream. Jews were making the desert bloom. It all had the makings of Hasidic song.

"A smart Jew," he had told Harry, "is a Jew that has a passport. But a really intelligent Jew is one who carries his passport on him at all times."

The torch had passed. Sam, successful in business in America, did not inculcate the old ways. They remained a kind of memory. Somewhere he kept a black fur hat in the closet, but he didn't make Harry wear it. Harry spent some time at yeshiva, but then transferred. Even the synagogue they still went to was more reformed than not. Harry was never ever made to feel he really needed a passport.

Sometimes he wondered if it was false complacency. He was no fool. He had heard school kids mutter "Christkiller." He knew that in Brookline a lot of them were Jews — but the U.S.A. was pretty good, too. Somehow the Oath of Allegiance, the Fourth of July, Thanksgiving, and even Christmas were mixed into his memory so that he had a place in a pluralistic universe.

The Rosevales had missed the Holocaust. A sort of gratefulness to America had replaced some of the bitterness of exile. Though Sam got a thrill from every goat and orange tree in the desert of the Holy Land, Harry felt some kind of comfort at being an American in a country of peace and prosperity, where the tanks and the rocks were not being hurled back and forth on the streets everyday. No green line. In fact, he thought of Israel as a sort of No Man's Land caught between powers, peoples, and religions. There Jews were indentured to a yoke of fate dictated mostly by the past, by ancestral inheritance.

These two views helped to form the difference between Sam and Harry. To Harry America was a comfortable, middle-class living room, with a refrigerator nearby and a TV box in front of the sofa, where one could peer undisturbed into the future. Judaism was a memory in comparison to this life, this liberty and pursuit of happiness — even though it contained some of his warmest memories: the Sabbath, for instance, the candles on Friday evening, the grace after dinner, Sam reading from the Torah, his own Bar Mitzvah. There was nothing, either, in America like the songs, the Hasidic songs that Sam would revive on occasion and Harry's mother, Miriam, would sing with such a clear, sweet voice. They had kept the candles and the Sabbath feast, and the synagogue on Saturday, but Harry hardly gave it a thought when he flicked on an electric light on the Sabbath before the three stars had appeared in the twilight sky marking the end of the day. The Rabbi's divinations were not his favorite thoughts, and he no longer read the Talmud or the Midrash. Whether or not to cook an egg on the Sabbath, and whether it would be a sin against God, did not enter into his thinking — although the Rosevales did, out of habit, put off washing the dishes until Saturday evening.

And now there was Rachel.

2 The Chinese Guitar

What would he tell little Rachel? That his religion was an outworn memory? Or that the Messiah was yet to come? When? Tomorrow? Or six thousand years from now? Or when God was ready, as tradition dictated? Did he even believe any longer in a personal Messiah? Or, like the reform Jews, was Redemption simply going to be a gradual salvation coming on without any personal savior? Rachel's smile was like a question mark to Harry, all the more so because she was a girl.

On the way home from the office one evening, Harry stopped in the village for some supplies. On the way back to his car, he passed Brentz's Music Shop, which was around the corner from the parking lot. There was the dust of snow on the pavements. It was almost the holiday season. Harry was thinking of the new baby, and he wondered if Rachel was the right name for her.

Why hadn't they been more imaginative? She could have been Deirdre, or Ephrat, or some name like *dawn of the morning*, a golden name. Rachel. Jacob's wife. What had

Rachel ever done but continue the blood line, tend the cows, see to the herd? Harry did not even know that Rachel had stolen the idols from her father's tent before she and Jacob broke camp with him. If he'd found out, he'd want to know why Rachel's father had idols anyway — they were forbidden, just like pork.

The music shop was dressed for the holidays. There were bright little castanets, tambourines, drums, trombones, trumpets, cymbals, gourds, violins, and guitars. "What if Rachel were a dancer?" the window seemed to say. Harry had never thought what his daughter might be, except a wife. He had married Deborah when she was eighteen.

Harry did know that he had always wanted to play the guitar. Not pops guitar, not folk guitar, but the classical guitar, the guitar of Spain. The rapid-fire staccato of the strings had always seemed to him the call of some fiery promise. It made him alert. And the lingering of the melody on the upper strings had always called to him as the epitome of tenderness. It was as if there was a gypsy in him somewhere that had never got out — cloak, shawl, hat, guitar, and all.

It was one of Harry's hidden fantasies, almost the only one, and in the window, hung beside a quarter-sized and a half-sized violin, he noticed a small brown guitar about the same size as Rachel. It had a neck, a little bottom, and plastic mother-of-pearl pegs. There was a little white nut, a black keyboard, brass frets, and a bridge up over the round hole. The rosette was a simple arrangement of concentric black circles. In the middle it said, *MADE IN CHINA - $27.*

Rachel would be a guitarist, Harry thought with excitement. He remembered her pudgy little fingers wrapping around his index finger. How long before she would be able to stretch those fingers over the guitar frets and pluck the strings with her thumb? Could he teach her? Did babies learn guitar like the violin, like the piano? Were there prodigies on the guitar like on other musical instruments? The idea excited Harry as he popped into Brentz's and bought Rachel her first guitar. Before she was even one! They put it in a shopping bag and Harry drove home proud of his new find.

"What's that?" asked Deborah.

"A guitar!" Harry answered, beaming.

"Why is it so small?" Deborah asked.

"It's for Rachel," Harry replied, holding it up. "Ole!"

Deborah blinked.

"She's going to be a guitarist," said Harry. "Probably the finest woman guitarist of this century. She can start having lessons right away. She can have it instead of a rattle."

"Harry, Rachel is all of two months old."

"Mozart was only four when he gave his first concert."

"Mozart played the piano. A child can't break a piano."

"We'll teach her how to hold it every day like a puppy. She's going to be a musician. No office hours. No dentistry school. No identity problem. A guitarist. And she'll wear one of those long black skirts and a stunning blouse and she'll travel to New York, London, Madrid, Jerusalem."

"What if Rachel doesn't want to be a guitarist?" Deborah asked. "Have you thought of that?"

Harry looked crestfallen. "Not want to be a guitarist? My girl?"

Deborah laughed, "Maybe she'll be a rabbi."

Harry winced.

She leaned into his arms. "You're incurable," she said. "A romantic after all. But what an idea. Jazz. Had you thought of jazz?"

"No," admitted Harry. "But I don't mind — as long as she learns Bach first. Think, Deborah. She's going to be famous."

"Her fingers have quite a lot to learn first, dear," said Deborah, and they went into Rachel's room together.

"I'll hang it above the crib," Harry said, strumming the six strings above Rachel's head. It was the first sound of the guitar for Rachel: strum… strum. But she didn't even wake up. And Harry hung the instrument up on the wall above her head. It looked like a still life, and Harry was pleased with his handiwork. But also serious. This was not a joke. It was an inspiration.

Suddenly Rachel woke and smiled.

3　The Amulet

When Rachel was four, Deborah put her in a preschool playgroup in the neighborhood. It was a mixed group. In fact, Deborah wanted it that way. She was pleased. She and Harry had talked about these things. They didn't feel that Rachel should be bound to an orthodox playgroup or that all the children had to be Jewish. After all, it was a free world. If it was a free world for adults, why not for children?

Deborah used to walk Rachel there. She dressed her in pink. Rachel's auburn hair had already grown to her shoulders. She was going to be a pretty girl — she was already an adorable baby. Maybe "adorable" was not exactly the right word for Rachel. She was pert. She could ask questions by the fistful. Deborah wondered if there would ever be an end to it. If she could ask so many questions at such a young age, like "Why is the moon blue, Mama?," what would become of her when she reached the age of reason?

Was asking questions especially Jewish? Deborah supposed it was. There were Einstein and Freud to think of. Perhaps asking questions was an existential answer to the identity crisis of modern Jews, and perhaps it explained why so many of them had come up with remarkable answers in this century. Deborah didn't see it as a religious problem, but perhaps it was even a reflection of the wandering of the Jews, of the Holocaust, of having to ask directions in so many strange places at such strange times.

To be a Jew was a question in itself, but Rachel asked why Harry left home every day, why the refrigerator was cold, why Deborah didn't have another man in the hours when Harry was away, why the sun was yellow, and why her name was Rachel. Besides, she was a vexingly reasonable little girl. Everything seemed to have a question and an answer was just the cause of another question. If the sun was yellow because it was hot, why was it hot? Because it was yellow?

Finally Deborah remembered the story her own grandfather had told her. What was at the end of the universe?

A door. And behind the door? Another door. And behind that door? A room. And in the room at the end of the universe was a man. He was sitting in a large armchair, smoking a giant cigar. The only trouble was that Harry didn't smoke. Dentistry had taught him what smoke does to the gums. But Deborah couldn't tell that to Rachel, not yet, so the questions went on from morning to night.

The playgroup was at a neighborhood house in Brookline. It was not a far walk for Deborah and Rachel. There were trees planted along the street. Trees were part of Rachel's fantasy of a playgroup. The trees were as much a part of the playgroup as the children.

"Why do the trees grow in the street?" asked Rachel. Deborah thought she might as well ask why the children grow in the playgroup.

It was that year that a girl called Melissa in the playgroup made friends with Rachel and gave her a crucifix. It was just a piece of costume jewelry about the size of a child's thumb, but one day when the two little girls were in a corner, Melissa took the crucifix from off her neck and gave it to Rachel.

Rachel had no Star of David to give Melissa. In fact, she wore a nametag around her neck. Rachel thought of giving Melissa her nametag in exchange for the crucifix, but somehow she thought Deborah would not be happy. Her mother had told her to show the nametag to someone if ever she got lost, so Rachel asked Melissa if she was supposed to show the crucifix to the policeman in case she got lost.

Melissa said, "No, it's just jewelry. It's supposed to be pretty."

And, in fact, it was pretty, made of blue enamel. Rachel took the crucifix home with her that day.

It was not a crucifix with the body of Christ on it, just the symbol of the cross. Rachel didn't know what it meant. She didn't even know it was supposed to mean anything. It might as well have been a leaf, for all it meant. But it meant something that Melissa had given it to her, and it meant something that it was pretty.

At home she showed it to Deborah, who asked her how she got it.

"Melissa gave it to me."

Deborah took the cross in her hand and looked at it pensively. She was reminded of the old Italian joke about the family that hung a cross in the home without a body on it because they were liberals. She shivered slightly. Were she and Harry also liberals? It was a poor joke; it was also a poor joke that Melissa had given this to Rachel.

To Deborah, the cross was like a sign of the barbarian, and she puzzled for a moment over the cruel, bare shape of the cross.

Oddly, she didn't think of Jesus but of the suffering of her own people. How much discrimination had been carried on in the name of this sign? Yet it looked like a scalpel, like an X, like a key. And to give it to a child!

"You have your own name tag," Deborah told Rachel, still clutching the blue enamel piece.

"Name tag?"

"For Rachel." Deborah made sure it was still around Rachel's neck.

"But it's not pretty," said Rachel.

"Not everything is pretty," answered Deborah, her fist closing around Melissa's blue cross. "This is not for you."

"Why not?"

Another question. "Because I say so," said Deborah, taking the cross away from her daughter's grasping hand.

"What about Melissa?" Rachel asked.

"I'll speak to her mother," answered Deborah.

The message Deborah got was very different from the message Rachel got. Deborah's reaction was one of irritation. It was just luck that one of the children would be wearing a cross and give it to Rachel. It could have happened to anyone. Still, Deborah could not help thinking that the cross should not have been there. Somehow it didn't belong in a child's playgroup. Then again, Rachel had probably asked, "What is it?" Someday Rachel would get into trouble with her bright little questions. That was Deborah's view. The world was a place that would not bear too much questioning.

But to Rachel the episode had a different meaning. It was one of the first incidents of life that she really remembered.

An encounter with a bauble. A pretty enamel cross, a blue cross that Mother took away from her. Rachel did not know its meaning. She was too young for meaning. It was not a symbol, not yet. All that Rachel learned was that, somehow, she was not good enough for a cross.

4   Garden City

At the end of the day Harry, after arriving home from the office, would take a few minutes to gather himself in the armchair and sip a glass of sherry. More often than not Deborah, with supper to cook and Rachel to look after, was too busy to join him. Harry took this time to gather himself from the day, go over what happened at the office, and see what his schedule with Deborah was for the evening.

Rachel was a little shy of Harry, but this evening she had a question. Besides, Deborah had said, "Ask Papa," so Rachel was approaching Harry's armchair coyly with one hand holding her skirt and circling up to the big man with her inquisitive eyes.

"So what is it Mopsy?" he said, seeing her approach.

"Papa," she said, a finger on her mouth as if she might ask him a special favor.

"Yes, Rachel."

"Papa, where is Jerusalem?"

Harry snorted. With a laugh, he said, "Why it's on the other side of the world."

"Is that far away?"

"Brookline is a long way from Jerusalem," Harry agreed.

"Then, Papa, if God lives in Jerusalem, why do we live in Brookline?"

Harry became serious. "We can't always live where God lives," he said. Rachel's face fell, and he immediately regretted the remark.   What he meant to say was that God lives everywhere. That would have been better.

Why hadn't he said that? Was it just a slip of the tongue, or did he secretly think that God doesn't live just everywhere? What about Brookline? He and Deborah had moved there because they called it Garden City   there was a Rosenblum on every corner. But he had never thought of it as God's place. He had never really questioned what it would mean to Rachel. But, after all, that mattered. Little children come from somewhere. To an adult it doesn't matter because they already come from somewhere else. But a child's home is its heaven.

"Jerusalem is an ancient city with a huge gold dome," said Harry lamely.

"Is that why God lives there?" Rachel said.

"God told Abraham to live there," Harry said. "And we're all descended from Abraham. Then King David built his temple there. That's where the Wailing Wall is."

"Why doesn't God live in Boston?" Rachel asked.

Harry snorted again. "Some people think he does," he said. "The Cabots. The Lodges. Cardinal Cushing."

Rachel's face fell again. "You mean he doesn't live in Jerusalem?"

"Once upon a time he lived in Jerusalem," Harry said.

"But he doesn't anymore?"

"No. I suppose he does."

Rachel pondered slightly. "Papa, why do we live in Brookline?"

It was Harry's turn to ponder. The office? Freedom and the pursuit of happiness? Because they were born there? Because of the housing? Or was it the Second World War? The ghetto. Immigration.

"You were born here, mopsy," Harry said, patting her cheek. "Ask your mother about that."

5　The Sabbath

It was Friday night. Deborah had the stuffed fish and the chicken noodle soup on the stove and the pot roast in the oven. There was wine from California. Rachel liked the Sabbath — or Shabbat, as Grandpa Sam called it. There was no oil lamp, but there were candles. There were no thirty-nine rules of prohibited actions, no *shabbas goy* — a non Jew employed by Jews on the Sabbath to perform tasks that they themselves were forbidden to do, like turning on electric lights.

In fact, Rachel could not say what was so special about the day — something in the attitude of Harry and Deborah, that was all. They made it a little special, out of nothing. Not even a Holy Night, but the end of the week. A niceness. Rachel had to be clean. Deborah put a new dress on her. Harry and Deborah treated each other kindlier. She had to watch what she said. The adults listened to each other. It was different from the other days in the week.

Sometimes Grandpa Sam and Miriam came. Sometimes there were other relatives. In Grandpa Sam's own childhood, orthodoxy was almost synonymous with ethnicity, a folkway of life. To Rachel, of course, those words meant nothing. But Grandpa Sam meant a lot. He was an icon. Transplantation to America had meant a change of life. It was the change of customs for a new ideology. Being a Jew became more theoretical. Perhaps this was true in the new land of Israel, too, but there they tried to reinforce the customs.

In America, instead, the teeming, bubbling life of the tenements consisted of all newcomers. It was as if they were all different denominations rubbing up against each other. In the old ghetto, it had been clear that secular education, modern social life, and modern music were all sins. Of course, that made them attractive. But America culture was a shibboleth, bubble gum was a mark of identity; the popular ways were a means by which the orthodoxy excommunicated the reformists — for chewing bubble gum.

In the old ghettos the rules had been the ways of the street; in the new world the rules were theoretical, perfunctory. They told you about them, but no one followed them. The rules were one thing, behavior another. America was the melting pot: one no longer had to stop driving on the Sabbath, one no longer had to wear a yellow star. Sam had to admit it — it was far from Jerusalem, even, where they not only danced the folk dramas but pinned posters on each other to say they were unkosher Jews.

In America, maybe there were no real Jews, no Sabbath. Except people sometimes pretended that they still knew the old ways. But they danced without the joy, without the roots — they had the freedom, but to be what? The irony was that one's neighbor was dressed in the same gray suit as oneself, drove the same car, lived in the same kind of house, but, theoretically, was conservative, not reform. "Dress British, think Yiddish."

Ideology was no longer based on the actualities of real life, the length of a beard, but on the pretences. For Jews, America was a land of echoes. Grandpa Sam saw them pretend to the light of the menorah, not because in America it was the real light of the soul — the electric bulb was that — but because the lost Jews still wanted to pretend to be Jews even though they were in the New World.

For Sam it was second nature not to mix milk and meat, or eat pork, crab, and shrimp. If his stomach didn't quite turn, his heart did. It was not revulsion but fastidiousness. It was a matter of taste, not an abstract rule.

For Harry, it was different. He was a second-generation Jew. Food rules seemed un-American, even silly. Harry didn't have it in his heart, like Sam, not to eat these things, but the rule still annoyed him. He felt guilty. It was a matter of his head. Though the head said no, his stomach said yes. For Harry the problem was one of not being instinctually part of a heritage. For Harry it was hard. It was artificial. America was full of artificial Jews, synthetic Jews.

For Rachel, his daughter, he knew it would all be different. She would associate lobsters with a good time. Breaking the taboos would be fun, fun. <u>Her</u> tummy and her head would both say yes, yes.

The Sabbath was a part of memory. It memorialized the rest enjoyed by God after the creation, and in the Ten Commandments, its observance was enjoined by God to commemorate his bringing the Israelites out of Egypt. In former times violation of the Sabbath was a capital offence. All this Harry knew, but it wasn't in his bones, like in Sam's. In fact, Harry tried to expel the long atavistic memory, the famous memory, but it stole through the backdoor of his dreams. If he turned on the television on Friday afternoon, he could not forget. He would think of Sam.

Harry's past was gone, but the ghost of memory survived.

A real American, instead, didn't have a past. All yesterday meant was the Revolution, and maybe the Civil War.

Yet, Harry, the assimilated Jew, envied Sam. He knew Sam remembered other things: the organ grinder with songs of piety, potatoes, and poverty. The marriage brokers under red umbrellas and wonder-working rabbis with amulets. He knew that Sam worried who, on his death, would find his body — an old person who could recite the Book of Psalms before his funeral?

In a sense, Sam's homeland died, but the past remained his home. Sam, with his old ways, could be as successful as an American in the stationery business, but on Friday night, to beguile time, he would play a record of "My Yiddishe Momme." The glazed Western world would fall away, and continents and time would merge. This memory saved his identity. Sam could strengthen himself from the fountain of nostalgia, while Harry's fountain of memory was not so strong — he had to rebuild.

Gradually, for Sam, the calculator replaced the finger beads. Occasionally he would sigh a blessing on Harry, but Harry had no blessings to give Rachel. For Harry, despite Sam's God, blessings seemed to come from the worldly world. Harry's inspirations seemed to have come more from the jukebox than the pulpit. A real Jew, Sam had told him, is someone who recites three services a day and a hundred blessings. If so, Harry wasn't a Jew, but he couldn't say so to Sam. He couldn't even think of a hundred things to bless.

He was a Jew without being religious. It was tiring. Harry had to make it all up, while to Sam the prayers were like old-fashioned duties — he knew them by heart. They refreshed him. Harry sometimes envied the old man his Yiddish and his orthodoxy because they meant Sam didn't have to create his own modernist piety. It would all be easier, thought Harry, if it <u>were</u> just a matter of the old prayer books, the ark, and the eternal flame. The trouble in America was that none of this came as a matter of course — you had to choose it, do it yourself. God came easier in the U.S.A., in one way, but in another way there was less of him.

"Well, by the great shining light," said Grandpa as he came in the door, "it's little Rachel. Song of songs. And how is the little one?"

"Fine," said Rachel, beaming.

"Have you lit the candles?"

"Not yet."

"What? No questions for Grandpa?"

"Oh, yes," said Rachel. She had a big question,

"What's the question?"

"What was Jesus?" Rachel looked up at him.

"This is the Sabbath," Grandpa scowled. "Moses said so."

"Was Jesus Moses' son?"

"Not exactly." Grandpa was a bit at a loss. He didn't think he could really tell Rachel the difference between the Sermon on the Mount and the giving of the Ten Commandments on Mount Zion. He couldn't say Jesus was a wise man or a troublemaker. "Where did you get this question?" Grandpa asked.

"From Melissa."

"I'll tell you what. I'll tell you the alphabet. Okay?"

"You're not going to tell me who Jesus was? I said I'd ask Grandpa."

Sam bundled her up in his arms and went into the living room. He thought he should say a Jew was somebody who always knew what not to do but never knew what to do. What not to say but not what to say — but that wasn't right, either. A Jew should always know what to say.

"Jesus died on a cross," Grandpa said.

"A cross?"

"A tree."

"You mean he lived in a tree?"

Grandpa laughed. "No, he died in a tree."

"Why didn't he come down?" Rachel asked.

"He was stuck there," said Grandpa.

"Stuck in a tree?"

"Well, he didn't want to be. The Romans put him there."

"Why didn't he call the fire department?"

"There was no fire department in those days."

"Didn't he starve to death?"

"Yes."

"He must have been hungry," said Rachel.

"He was," said Sam. "He was a human person."

"Is that what I tell Melissa?"

"Yes. Now what's the first word of the alphabet?"

"'Aleph.' It stands for God."

"Right. And then?"

"Bet. It stands for creation."

"Right."

"I forget the rest. Grandpa, was Jesus a Jew?"

"Ahem," said Sam. "You know what Hebrew means? What Jew means? It means 'someone from the other side of the river.'"

"Was Jesus from the other side of the river?"

"Well, yes. Definitely yes. Very much the other side of the river."

"Which river?"

"The Jordan."

"Are we from the other side of the river?"

"Yes," said Sam, scratching his head. "But not from the same side of the river as Jesus."

"Oh," said Rachel.

6   The Donkey

At the meal, with the kosher food, when Sam, Miriam, Harry, and Deborah were talking about the week, Rachel looked on contentedly. Somehow these people being together was what made Sabbath. More than prayers, the synagogue, the rabbi, the Torah, the ark — it was wholly unidentifiable. "Spiritual" would have been the word, if she had known it. The spirit. It was not the ark, the Book — those were things. For Rachel, young as she was, it was these people that were ineffable. Like the candle flames.

When they passed the pot roast, Rachel asked, "What was the donkey called?"

"What donkey?" asked Harry. Sometimes, on Saturdays, Grandpa Sam took Rachel to the zoo.

Rachel looked at Grandpa Sam. He shrugged.

"The donkey that brought Jesus into Jerusalem," said Rachel.

"Oh, really," said Deborah. "If you're going to be cute, you can go to your room." She turned to Sam, "Melissa sets her up." Then to Rachel, "Why don't you play with Judy Kaplan?"

"Judy's father is a *rynecologist*," said Rachel. She remembered the word because it was like rhinoceros.

"What's wrong with a donkey? There's nothing bad about a donkey," Harry said to Deborah.

"What was his name?" Rachel insisted.

"You tell Melissa he was called Moses," said Harry.

"Harry!"

"Moses? But Moses created the world." Rachel looked puzzled.

"That's right," said Harry.

"Abraham," said Sam.

"God," said Deborah. "Yahweh."

"God can't be the donkey," said Harry.

They all burst out laughing. They couldn't help it. God as the donkey was too much for them, and Rachel burst out laughing, too. Apparently it was some joke, and Rachel was happy. Even Deborah winked her wink at her, which usually she did when the men were being solemn or talking about politics. Rachel couldn't wait to tell Melissa.

"You tell Melissa the donkey was called Quixote," said Deborah. "Tell her it was a kosher donkey. And ask her who Cervantes was."

7   The Birthday

Rachel's ties to Grandpa Sam were what a child, later in life, dreams of — Sam was jovial, whereas Harry was brooding. It was his Jewishness, too. Grandpa wasn't something else. He was just Grandpa. He still had the accent, the trace of the stetl; he couldn't be anything else even if he wanted to. Harry, instead, could be an American. It was confusing. He had a choice. He could acculturate. He could assimilate. But Sam was stuck with what he was. Sam was happy to have made it in America. He didn't have a bad word for his new land, but the treasure of the old world was his, too. Sometimes it seemed as if Sam had both worlds while Harry had neither, and when he showed up with Miriam, Rachel was extra happy to jump into his lap.

It was her birthday. She was six. It was also Passover, the feast celebrating the Jewish passage from slavery to freedom. The Haggadah, the ritual service performed in the home on the first Passover evening, states, "And if the Holy One, praised be He, had not taken our ancestors out of Egypt, then we, and our children, and our children's children, would still be enslaved to Pharoah in Egypt. Now even if all of us were scholars, all of us sages, all of us elders, all of us learned in Torah, it still would be our duty to tell the story of the Exodus from Egypt. And whoever expands upon this story of the Exodus deserves praise."

It was called Pesah — Passover. Harry and Deborah didn't celebrate a real seder, but they made an informal one. Most of it was up to Grandpa.

"So," he said as he came in, "the little one is six." And Rachel jumped up on his legs.

"And what day is it?" Grandpa asked.

"My birthday," said Rachel.

"Passover," said Grandpa.

Rachel took him by the hand and showed him the table.

"The salt water is for the tears of the slaves," she said, "and the matzoth is the bread of affliction."

Grandpa smiled.

"What is affliction?" Rachel asked.

"Rachel, Rachel," said Grandpa. "Affliction is what the Jews had in Egypt."

Then he held her fast and told her, "Rachel, God comes with laughter. You know, when the children of Israel reached the Red Sea, they didn't know what to do. But they were being pursued. Chased. So one started pushing and said, 'You go first.' And another pushed and said, 'You go first,' and they all started pushing each other until someone fell into the Red Sea, and that was how the waters were parted."

Rachel said, "And that's what Passover is?"

Grandpa laughed.

"And not my birthday?"

Grandpa pulled out a present wrapped with ribbons. "That's for your birthday," he said.

"Oh, goody," said Rachel as she took the present. She unwrapped it on Grandpa's knees.

"It's a ragamuffin doll!" she cried, and Grandpa Sam beamed.

She hugged it. Then she asked, "Grandpa, what is a rabbi?"

"Grandpa smiled. "A rabbi is a teacher with a long black coat on," he said.

"Really?" Rachel asked with big eyes.

"Really," said Grandpa.

"What about Jesus? Was he a rabbi?" Rachel asked.

Deborah came up just then to greet Sam. "A ragamuffin doll. Oh, Rachel, how lucky you are!"

But Rachel looked at Sam and said, "Jesus was a Christian rabbi." She smirked, as Melissa had done in the playgroup when she told Rachel about Jesus.

"Nonsense," said Deborah. "Now you let Grandpa go. You have to give a name to your doll."

"I'll call him Jesus," said Rachel.

Deborah frowned. Grandpa looked slightly bewildered.

"Jesus was a man," said Deborah. "He's dead. You can't call a ragamuffin that. Call her Molly."

"Molly?" said Rachel.

"Rachel learns such nonsense in the playgroup," Deborah apologized. "I'm thinking of keeping her home."

Rachel looked at her mother. "But I want to show Molly to Melissa," said Rachel. "Maybe Molly can play with Jesus."

"Hush, now," said Deborah, "you don't know what you're saying. The table is ready."

8　The Zoo

That afternoon Grandpa took Rachel to the zoo. It was already slightly spring, officially spring, but the weather had warmed only a little. Still, the animals were outside. Lots of other children were there in their winter coats, tugging their parents' hands. It was almost the season for flowers, and the animals were taking their first stretch. The zebra, the giraffe, the lama, the camel, the lemurs, the monkey, the bears. It was a merry community.

They came to the orangutan.

"Grandpa," said Rachel as they watched the monkey watching them. "Don't you think he looks like Papa?"

"What a thing to say," said Grandpa. "Harry isn't hairy. Harry doesn't walk on his hands. What makes you say such a thing?"

"His eyes."

She was silent for a while. The orangutan was peeling a banana. "Grandpa, do they ever put people in cages?"

"No," said Grandpa, after a pause.

"Not even Jews?" asked Rachel.

Grandpa's smile disappeared. "Who told you that?" he asked.

"Melissa."

Grandpa sighed. "It wasn't a zoo," he said.

"What was it?" asked Melissa. "Were you in a cage?"

"It was war," Grandpa said. "They were called concentration camps."

"Were you in one?"

"No. Miriam and I escaped."

"Is that why you're here?"

"Yes."

"What happened to the others? Did the children come and look at them on the Sabbath?"

"No. They died."

"Didn't they feed them?"

"No.. They killed them."

"What for?"

What was the answer? Because they were Jews? What was a Jew? Because they were God's chosen or because they denied God? Because they were not Aryan — blue-eyed and white skin? Or because they lived in ghettoes, prayed on Saturday, and ate no pork or shellfish? Because they loaned money? Because they were guilty — or because they were innocent?

"It's a long story, Rachel," said Grandpa, with a slight weariness.

"Does it have a happy ending?" she asked.

"I don't know," said Grandpa. "Now what else is bothering you?"

"What's a minyan, Grandpa? Why can't a girl be part of a minyan?"

"A minyan is a quorum. A majority. You can't have a prayer group without a minyan. But you have to be a boy."

"Don't girls count? Is that why God built the concentration camps?"

"No. The girls count in the home. But not in the law."

Rachel watched the orangutan with the banana.

"Grandpa, is that why I'm not circumcised? Because of the law?"

Grandpa laughed. He wanted to say, No, it's because you don't have a banana. But he shook his head gravely. "Yes, Rachel, it's because of the law."

9   Dr. Themagorsky

Rachel had just turned twelve when she saw her first film clips of Hiroshima and Nagasaki. These are interesting documents. One might think they would amuse a twelve-year-old, what with the mushroom blast and the smoke. Children love to play with fire. Here are a couple of celluloid clips that, like toys, Americans can play over and over again, producing images of powder puffs and belching power to a child's delight. It is like the ideal explosive toy. With a button, any American child can explode 100,000 Japanese bodies into nothing. Into an oblivion of yellow dust. A smudge on a screen. What power! What glory!

They didn't amuse Rachel. She turned ashen white and asked Harry, "What's that?" How was he to explain? That other than Hitler's final solution for the Jews, than Stalin's genocide in Russia, these pictures were witness to the single greatest crime against humanity ever committed by mankind? How was a child of twelve to grasp that? How was she to understand that the leaders of America, the nice man in the hat with the smile, the man from Missouri, Harry

Truman, married to Bess, father of Margaret, our homespun President, the man fighting evil for democracy, the right to life, liberty, and the pursuit of happiness, and happy Jimmy Byrnes, the people from next-door, the purveyors of apple pie and Coca-Cola, had dropped this monster in a village of men, women, and children?

Rachel rose at school for the American flag, yet she had to learn that this flag would permit the obliteration of hundreds of thousands of people, not even military targets, at the push of a button — why had they not dropped the bomb on an isolated mountain top, an uninhabited forest, a deserted island? All they needed to do was show the explosion, prove they had the bomb, without killing the people to prove their point.

Instead, the Americans, the great champions of fair play, of neighborly living, of good intentions to others, in one stroke had committed the greatest crime possible against humanity without even trying out a demonstration first to ward it off. What kind of people were Americans? What kind of land did she live in? If Americans were capable of this kind of savagery when a perfectly viable alternative plan was available — to blow up an isolated mountain, Mt. Fuji, in Japan — then perhaps everything else the Germans, the Japanese, and the Russians charged against the Americans was true. The episode threw the little girl into a depression. She could not face her teachers without thinking that they stood up for mass murder. She could not see the policemen in the streets without thinking that they were responsible for killing little Japanese boys and girls.

Harry sniffled. "It was war, Mopsy. There was a war."

"Why didn't they drop it on Mt. Fuji?"

"I don't know. The Japanese were killing Americans."

"They would have stopped," said Rachel. "How can I be an American?"

Harry shifted uncomfortably. "Yeah, well, that's the German problem, too. How can a German be a German?"

"But the Germans know they were wrong," said Rachel. "Americans don't know that they were wrong. Why not? Why doesn't the textbook say America was wrong to have dropped the bomb?"

"Not everything is in the textbooks," said Harry.

"Well, how is a child supposed to behave?" Rachel pouted.

Rachel stopped eating. Deborah and Harry were at wit's end. For a while she stopped playing guitar. Harry actually entertained the idea of sending Rachel to Israel and discussed it with her.

She looked at him glumly. "I'd go to Israel," she said, "but they're working on the bomb, too. They want to drop it on the Arabs to wipe out the seed of Amalek."

Harry couldn't laugh. All he could do was call Dr. Thermagorsky, a psychoanalyst, and make an appointment for Rachel. For some reason, Rachel went willingly. She saw the doctor alone.

"So what is this now that disturbs you?" he asked, like a father — a rabbi almost. "Something about the bomb?"

Rachel began crying. "How can I be a human being? How can we live after what we did? You were there. How could you permit it?"

"A doctor is not in charge of war," said Dr. Thermagorsky. He was a big, burly man with a partially bald pate and tufts of white and gray curls over his ears. He had a distinguished gray beard, neatly trimmed, and wore spectacles.

"We are a nation of murderers," said Rachel.

Dr. Thermagorsky lowered his eyes and wiped his spectacles. "You weren't even born, child," he said softly.

"What's wrong with everybody?" Rachel asked.

Dr. Thermagorsky did not know where to begin. "Do you want to be a doctor?" he asked.

"No. I'm a guitarist," said Rachel.

"Then that's how you can help," said Dr. Thermagorsky.

"How?"

"By playing your guitar."

Rachel thought of the powerpuff of bodies and little yellow ghosts floating above Hiroshima and imagined herself playing music as the mushroom expanded.

"You don't help the children by not eating, you know," said Dr. Thermagorsky.

"The music is too late," said Rachel.

"Someday you can go to Japan and play a benefit for Hiroshima," said the doctor, "but first you must eat. In some ways it is easier to be dead than alive. Life gives you responsibilities. You have to overcome. Go to the cemetery, Rachel. Take some flowers. Promise you will play them a song."

There was silence between them. There was not a great deal the doctor could do. Treating disease was one thing, but doctoring reality was another.

"Promise?"

Rachel folded her hands despairingly in her lap. "...promise," she said.

"You won't be sorry," the doctor said. "There is more mystery in life and death than we can fathom at any one time."

"But I hold you to account," Rachel said.

"Yes," he sighed. "That is right. And remember me at the graveyard."

10   The Funeral

The long, thin, simple wooden coffin spoke volumes to Rachel. Inside was old Sam — Grandpa. She thought he never deserved to die; in fact, that he was immortal. Sam, alive, was her very concept of immortality. She didn't need an abstraction to offer the life to come because Sam was it. It came with a sense that as long as he was there, she would be also. This was natural. He was a flower on the stem, and she was a little flower on a side stem. She never thought he could be, well, simply gone. Sam the answerer. He had always been there when she had questions, and he had survived so much that the question of his death had never occurred to her.

Even so, for Rachel, the funeral service at the synagogue was as if the past were a great poet, the poet Judaism, yet as if this poet of four thousand years had lost its audience, modernity, in the dust of ashes and assimilation.

The simple pine wood touched her. But Sam himself was silent. He lay inside the box of a secret, and he was not there to answer the question of his own death.

The whole family was on hand. Harry and Deborah, Rachel, Aunt Dvorska, her cousins Mosh and Ash, Mort Solomen — Grandpa's business partner, the Eislers, the Kaplans with Judy and everybody else, including the Hevra Kaddisha, the "holy brotherhood." It all seemed unlike Grandpa, as if someone else had taken over, and he had gone away. A place of no destination. The final wandering of the Jew.

At the end of the service they all stood and faced East to Jerusalem and said mourners' kaddish, the prayers for the dead. Rachel suddenly felt funny facing Jerusalem, wondering if now that he was no longer in the United States if Grandpa had gone there, to the Holy Land. He didn't seem the type. He had never been there when he was alive, why should he go there now that he was dead? She had heard her father's joke that more dead Americans go to the Holy Land to be buried than go when they are alive, but Grandpa's spirit had always been right here. The kaddish closed with the praise and glorification of God and hope for the establishment of God's kingdom on earth.

That made Rachel think. If they were hoping for the establishment of God's kingdom on earth that meant the earth was not God's kingdom. If this was not God's kingdom, whose was it? Grandpa Sam, in his simple wood coffin, was silent. There was no one to answer her question. Did the world belong to the rabbis? Or the Americans? Or the police? Who was at large here? If creation was not God's, whose was it?

This made the coffin and the lamentations and the mourning more sinister to her. Someone was at work, and it wasn't God.

Besides, what would the kingdom of God on earth be like? What would change? Would she still recognize Harry and Deborah? Would they all go to Jerusalem? Would the Temple on the Mount still be a big, beautiful, Arabic Dome?

She was looking at the rabbi as she thought this, wondering what Sam would answer, were he not silent, when she remembered their spelling game, when Sam kept saying, "Just add a 't' Rachel." For the longest time she couldn't get it as he made a "t" by crossing a finger off the top with his two index fingers. "T." Finally he pronounced it for her, "Rabbit" — and she learned to spell two words at once, "rabbi" and "rabbit." The whole secret of spelling in one lesson.

She always thought afterwards of rabbis as kinds of rabbits dressed in black, and it seemed to her that Bugs Bunny must in some way be Jewish.

Yet the funeral was grand in its way, too. Rachel had been a flower girl at a wedding, and the funeral reminded her most of that. In fact, she wanted it all for herself, jumbled together — the coffin, the mourning, the canopy, the "rabbit," the groom, the breaking of the glass underfoot, the singing, the folk dancing. From the synagogue they went by car to Mount Auburn Cemetery and filed into the area where the most Jews were buried, the "ghetto of the dead." The ground was already frozen. There was ice around the grave. It was cold. They hovered around the edge of the hole in the ground like black, fallen leaves looking for some place to blow away. Rabbi Solovetch had come with them from the synagogue.

After Sam was lowered, Rabbi Solovetch was supposed to say a few words and shovel in the first earth. "O, Israel. . .," he began, intoning for a while. Rachel wondered why they didn't sing, "God Bless America," the fine Jewish song by Irving Berlin that Harry loved, but she knew she was still small and didn't understand everything. Grandpa Sam, what would he have said?

Then Rabbi Solovetch, looking like a dumpling, finished and took the shovel. How Rachel disliked this man. He was so squat, dark, mysterious, and authoritarian. He scared and amused her at the same time. She had an almost morbid fascination with him as he dug the spade into the nearby earth. He seemed to be a living ritual. His black hat was back on his head and then suddenly it tipped and fell off into the grave. Rabbi Solovetch lunged after it with his free hand but slipped on the ice and tumbled, hat, coat, shovel, and all, into the grave.

There was a thud as he hit the coffin and a muffled outcry from the little black audience that gathered around. Rachel herself was touched by a certain glee. She had never seen anything as startling as the dignified little rabbi slipping and tumbling over his hat into the open grave. He was on his back stretching a hand up but nobody could reach him. Climbing out of a grave was not as easy as falling in, and no more dignified. Rabbi Solovetch was not athletic, either. He was tangled in his robes of black bombazine and trying to reach his velvet hat. He peered up at the mourners, who were extending their hands down to him, and he had to stand on the coffin.

Though she felt like it, Rachel did not giggle. She wondered if the rabbi would say a psalm down there. Finally one of the gravediggers got a sling and hauled him up. Someone had gotten a flask of brandy and gave him a gulp.

He was all right. They began to fill in the grave. The earth splattered on the coffin top and made a hollow sound.

Suddenly Rachel experienced something she would not recognize for a long time; she did not know it then, but it was a prophetic sympathy with God. It was not just the joke of seeing Rabbi Solovetch fall into the grave, but Sam's disappearance. It was not an emotion or an ecstasy, and she was still a child, but it was an openness and responsiveness to God's word itself. In a small way, it was the experience that, with Grandpa Sam gone, God had come. It was not like Moses in Sinai encountering God in an I and Thou relationship. Rachel did not think, because of her Jewishness, of God as the Son incarnated. A rebirth. But it was something. She sensed her own openness, her own receptivity — that was the coming of God.

Then Rachel, in the shadow of Sam's death, felt herself sway between unlimited possibilities and limited capacities, between a simultaneous denial and affirmation of self — necessity and freedom, anxiety and hope, fear of God and love of God. She was a small girl and these were big words, but it was like being at a circus and seeing that the clown was not only a clown but also a man. She wanted to ask Grandpa, if she could have phrased it, how, if she were to shun the law, to avoid statutes and principles, in a word, if she were going to live a modern life without the 638 rules of the Torah, the ritual, and the purification, how was she going to have an identity, a Jewish identity, or any identity? Wouldn't she be like Rabbi Solovetch in ecclesiastical dress stumbling into an open grave? Only she wouldn't be funny, because she was just a girl. And they would shovel the earth in and bury her alive.

Some people were Democrats or Republicans. Presumably they followed a code to be so. Christians were baptized and confirmed. But she? She wasn't even circumcised. How, if the openness of God became her angel, how would she identify — would she lose her Jewishness? If she lost her Jewishness, would she lose her mother and father — like she had lost Grandpa Sam? If there were no law, what would categorize her? Was this why the Jews of Germany, in the face of death, had even accepted the yellow star? To identify?

11 Bar Mitzvah

Rachel had heard of a bar mitzvah often enough, but she didn't really know what it meant. All she knew was that it was something that happens — but happens to somebody else. It was not supposed to happen to her. She did not know that it meant "Son of the commandment." She only knew it didn't happen to girls. Not to her.

She was jealous. Not of attaining legal and religious maturity. These were things that had not dawned on her yet. But she knew the boys were being prepared for something special, and she was not part of it. This was why, in class one day, she stole Jerry Eisler's bar mitzvah manual.

It was easy. Jerry was playing while Rachel was sitting there at the next desk. It had his name on it: "My Bar Mitzvah Book." The bold black letters begged for Rachel's attention. She tiptoed to his empty desk, looked around, and then slipped the manual into her own notebook. Nobody had noticed.

Harry had not wanted a bar mitzvah for Rachel — the ceremony concocted in the 1920s by reform Jews in America for girls. He considered it to be a commercialization. It didn't even seem dignified to Harry. He was too steeped in Sam's traditions to take much to innovation, and when it came to practice, Sam's old world orthodoxy still held the upper edge. Adaptations didn't feel real to Harry, even if in belief, intellectually, he was a liberal, reform Jew. The truth was Harry went by the watered-down rituals, but he hadn't given up belief in the old practices, either. He just didn't practice. He respected the skull cap, but he would never wear one. A skull cap meant real Jewry to him. But he himself was a subjective Jew. If he couldn't have Sam's old ghetto, he wouldn't have some pallid modern imitation, either. So Rachel would just have to go without a bar mitzvah. Girls singing the Torah. It was ridiculous.

But Rachel had her own ideas and was full of curiosity. So when she saw Jerry Eisler's bar mitzvah manual on top of the desk, she took it. It didn't feel like theft right away. She at first felt an exhilaration, as if she were appropriating something that belonged to herself. There was a surreptitious thrill about taking Jerry's manual, as if bar mitzvah really belonged to her. It did not matter that Harry and Deborah had planned something else for her, a debut on the guitar, a small public concert with a sort of festive kiddush and a catered reception afterwards — all for her. She was very excited about this, too, though scared; but it was not the same as a bar mitzvah.

That evening she sprawled on her bed with Jerry Eisler's bar mitzvah manual. The booklet began from the back. That at first made it seem forbidden, and slowly Rachel began to realize that she had done something wrong. It was the

Hamaftir series. The heavy black clear type in the lamplight seemed foreboding and admonitory. But she read on over the letters that she didn't understand, and it somehow seemed very wise and profound.

There were big words, impressive, like "compulsory" and "benediction," and pictures of the coils of the phylacteries, called the tephillin. They looked spooky, like thongs or handcuffs, but they were there to remind the wearer to keep the law.

It was then, as she read, that Rachel first realized she had actually stolen. The manual said conversation was prohibited, whatever that meant, during the putting on of the tephillin, and it was all very mysterious. There was one thong for the head and one for the arm and one for the finger. Rachel began to realize she had done something very wrong. The big black Hebrew letters accused her.

It said if the tephillin should fall on the floor while putting them on, the wearer would atone by fasting an entire day or by giving to charity.

This, though she knew nothing about atonement and cantillation, impressed her, and she wondered what Rabbi Solovetch would say if he knew that she had stolen Jerry Eisler's bar mitzvah manual. Atonement. That was another word she didn't know, but she knew it had something to do with her. It said that God is one. It said to keep the commandments. It said that God has redeemed us from Egypt and promised us the Holy Land. It said God rewards the pious and punishes the wicked. And all this was supposed to be Jerry's. Why couldn't girls know this, too? She didn't know why not. She only knew that an impulse to share in the bar mitzvah had made her do something awful, but she read on.

The part called the Haftorah was in English. It was called the conclusion, and it was very beautiful. Rachel couldn't imagine Jerry chanting this, and, in fact, it seemed to have more to do with her than with Jerry. "Arise, shine; for thy light is come, and the glory of the Lord shines upon thee."

She thought of her guitar. This part was romantic, and Rachel was awestruck. It said, "And thine heart shall stand in awe and be enlarged; because the abundance of the sea shall be converted unto thee, the wealth of nations shall come unto thee."

Rachel thought of the sea coming unto her. It all seemed wonderful and forbidden. She was glad she had stolen the booklet. It said, "The multitude of camels shall cover thee, the dromedaries of Midian and Ephrah; all of them from Sheba shall come; they shall bring gold and incense; and they shall show forth the praises of the Lord."

Rachel began to dream of camels. And all the flocks of Kedar, and the rams of Nebaioth. It was wonderful. Why hadn't Harry told her about this? Grandpa Sam would have known. But then she realized she could never share her secret. She wondered, "Who are these that fly as a cloud, and as the doves to their windows?" But there was no one to ask. No one to share it with. Then she heard a sound in the hall and the guilt electrified her heart. She jumped up and stuffed the manual in her drawer with her comic books and shut off the light.

She would always remember that moment later when she was a woman, and in the dark she felt she had wronged Jerry Eisler. She, a girl, had taken away something that belonged to him. She felt the wrong. And later as a woman she knew that contrition had touched her. Often, as a guitarist, when her guitar seemed to go silent and stop singing, she wondered if it was because she had done something wrong. Like taking Jerry Eisler's bar mitzvah manual. She would wonder if it was because she had sinned against Judaism. Just as she buried her face in the pillow that evening and wondered about the camels and the flocks of Kedar. Would she ever see them? Particularly since she had stolen the bar mitzvah manual? And she realized later that it was contrition that first touched her guilty heart then, when she was twelve, but she would also wonder how one can ever learn contrition without doing wrong.

KNOW WHO IT IS BEFORE WHOM YOU STAND.

12   The Debut

Rachel's guitar debut was after that. It was at the social center of the Sidney Kunowitz Synagogue. Harry thought of it as an alternative to a bar mitzvah. Harry, in his way, was trying to be modern, and the child, in her way, was a prodigy. Tilly Torqhardt, the guitar teacher, was skeptical, not because Rachel couldn't play but because she was so young. Somehow Tilly didn't favor this kind of exposure, but when she learned the details, she gave in. There would only be fifty or seventy-five people there. It would be on a Friday night. And they would celebrate a kiddush after the child played. Harry was pleased with himself.

There was, after all, an alternative to straight and pure religion. It was the guitar. In Harry's mind culture was the answer to many problems. Art was the alternative. It got around the direct confrontation with God and avoided the theological questions. There was a mystery about art. You didn't need to answer the question, "Is there a personal God?" Art didn't make you squirm. Like prayer, it was a discipline and a devotion, but it wasn't embarrassing. It didn't put you on the spot, like religion.

Rachel was very excited. She had a new dress, a blue velvet affair with a black lace collar and a pink sash. She had tried it on in the mirror and liked herself. She was too young for dances but having the recital was like going to a dance. She was coming out. She put her old clothes into the closet like vanished selves and looked forward to Friday evening as if it were her true self about to emerge.

She sat down at her little writing table that week, and in a new notebook she printed in large caps:

RACHEL ROSEVALE

CONCERT GUITARIST

There was going to be a printed program with her name on it and the pieces she was going to play, and a little quote, a précis, from her guitar teacher, Tilly Torqhardt.

She was also busy practicing her pieces, the Canary Jig, also known as Canarios, a popular dance of the seventeenth century thought to be based on a dance of the natives of the Canary Islands. This was the easiest piece. Then there were two etudes, one in D, by Fernando Ser, and the other in B-minor. They were mostly melody and arpeggio, and she had practiced them hundreds of times. She would also play Robert de Visee's *Allemand*, which was the hardest piece, and she liked it the least even if he had been the guitarist of Louis XIV and had played at court. But it was the one Tilly worked her hardest on because of the stretches at the third and fifth frets. Then there were three songs. It was quite a lot for a little girl, even if it did last only twenty minutes or so.

Although her hand was still small, her fingers had matured and she was musical by nature. Tilly had no problem with her at all. Harry's faithful sessions with her in her crib hugging the guitar and strumming it over and over had paid off, too, and the half-guitar he had bought her as a baby still hung on the wall.

Tilly Torqhardt was a redhead. She had won Rachel over by being her friend and confidante as well as her guitar teacher. There was something impetuous about Rachel that Tilly liked, and she had high hopes for her as a guitarist. She only worried that Rachel's hand was a little small, and she wondered if the girl would grow out a little. On the other hand, Segovia was pudgy. So was the guitar teacher Sophocles Pappas. She didn't worry. She even taught Rachel Spanish as they went along. The one thing Tilly abhorred was the guitar as a bump-and-grind instrument. No other instrument had such a split personality as the guitar, but she hoped Rachel would develop a flamenco, rather than a pick, interest in the guitar, or at least a Latin style, before getting tempted by popular music in her teens. Quietness, concentration, and the lullaby effect were Tilly's trademarks. Songs and scales, scales and songs.

Harry told Rachel that the guitar debut was instead of a bar mitzvah, so Rachel took the event very seriously. She realized the music was partly her obligation to God. She understood that it was instead of the law. This meant it was not just a theatrical event, but some of the excitement caught her anyway, whereas the seriousness of it helped her to offset stage fright. That was until Friday. Then she got the jitters, and, believing she couldn't go through with it, she went to her room and cried.

Deborah followed her into her room.

"What is it, honey?" she said.

Rachel was looking at her new dress. "It's so beautiful," she said, the tears trickling down her cheeks.

"So why cry?"

"I can't do it," Rachel answered. "I can't remember the notes."

"But you've done it hundreds of times," Deborah said, sitting down on the bed beside her.

"Mama? Were you ever afraid?"

"Everybody is afraid sometimes."

"What if I make a mistake?"

"Mistakes don't matter," said Deborah. "Tilly will be there. You just go on."

"I never thought it would be this way. I thought it would be like when we heard Segovia. A big hall. A hush. Lights. Hundreds of people. I never thought it would be just me."

"It's not just you," said Deborah. "It's Tilly and Harry and Fernando Sor and Segovia and Robert de Visee. It's all of us."

"You'll be there, won't you?" Rachel asked, looking up. "My new dress looks good, doesn't it, Mama? But next year it will already be too small. It's sad to think. I'll need a new guitar, too. Papa said he would get me a concert guitar. But it's still sad. I don't see why I have to grow up, do you?"

Deborah laughed. "Being old is fun," she said, even though it was partly a lie. That was the thing; Rachel didn't need to lie yet. You could even hear it when she played the guitar. Each note was sweet and pure. Playing wasn't yet a trick for her.

The same had been true of the *Nutcracker*. For several years now Rachel had been taking ballet classes. They helped her with her music. One, two, three, four. The counting got into her limbs. It made more sense when you knew that the music was a dance and that all the concentration of the fingers was like a taut, wound-up body. Then they put her in the Boston Ballet's *Nutcracker* with the children — the Aronson, Bernstein, Bloomberg, Cohen, Dahin, Fink, Gelfand, Goldstein, Hoffman, Irwin, Kline, Lichtman, Pearlman, Silverstein, Warner, and Zinkevich girls. To be fair, there were a lot of Wasp, Nordic, and Chinese girls in the children's chorus, too, but even so, Rachel was confused.

"Is the *Nutcracker* Jewish?" asked Rachel.

Deborah laughed.

"I mean, how come the Silberhauses have a Christmas tree?"

"They're Viennese," said Deborah, while Harry was listening.

"The mice are Christian," said Harry.

"Harry!"

Rachel was one of the children under Mother Ginger's skirts, one of the polichinelles. Big Mother Ginger was a man, who they all made fun of. But what interested Rachel most was the elaborate illusion — of the Christmas tree growing bigger, of Dr. Drosselmeyer's nutcracker becoming a real soldier, of the mice in the night, the snow in the Christmas tree forest, and the illusion of clouds and mist.

It was the difference between illusion and reality that caught her attention, like the way the ballerinas she saw in their street clothes were suddenly transformed into snow queens, snowflakes, and sugar plum fairies. So many of the dancers were Jewish, yet illusion itself didn't seem Jewish. It wasn't the same as the Hanukkah stories that always had reality, pain, and sorrow mixed in with the lights.

"It's a kind of magic," Deborah told her.

"Is it the same as the guitar?" Rachel asked.

"It could be," Deborah said. "Someday you could play something as magical on the guitar as the dances of coffee, tea, and marzipan."

"And the *Waltz of the Flowers*," said Rachel.

Yet still the power of illusion puzzled her. She did not really know it until she got older, but it was one of the time-honored questions of the theater — is it real or fake, moral or Christian? That was why she asked if it was Jewish. There was always an element *of* realism, a moral message, a way of life about Jewish stories that Tchaikovsky seemed to have transcended in E.T.A. Hoffmann's tale. Rachel couldn't identify with Clara because she thought it sort of silly to float around in a balloon, so she assumed Clara was Christian. But Hoffmann the writer must have been Jewish. And Silberhaus, too, and Dr. Drosselmeyer. Yet everything was tinsel and gold and Christmassy, so it was confusing. Yet she loved the illusion. And she hoped one day she would be able to give an illusion like that with the guitar, like Tilly Torqhardt when she played the tremolo with her three butterfly fingers from the *Recuerdos de las Alhambra*.

Part Two

13 First Blood

Blood came suddenly, a little trickle between her legs. She was visiting Judy Kaplan, and she told her. Judy was excited.

"That's your period," she said gleefully. "You're a woman now. Pretty soon you'll need a diaphragm."

It didn't appear so womanly to Rachel. She wondered if it had something to do with being Jewish or kosher. Or unkosher.

It seemed to make her feel slightly guilty, she didn't know for what. It was blood, after all; everything was based on blood. Blood was the story of mankind. Now, suddenly, she was somehow a part of it. A secret history.

Judy loaned her a napkin and asked her if she felt all right. She didn't notice a thing except the blood. It was the involuntariness of it that was incongruous. It made her feel slightly giddy, too, and she wanted to lie down, but Judy wanted to make her some warm tea.

So Rachel was no longer a girl. Not by tradition. According to orthodoxy, or at least tradition, she was ready to have babies and it was time to marry. In the old world she wouldn't have had much more time to wait.

They talked. "It's only menstruation," said Judy. "I mean, it's not a dirty thing. Even if they say we are unclean and can't go to temple. And you can't touch your man during the days you bleed. Isn't it silly?"

Rachel didn't know if it was silly. It was a little uncomfortable and inconvenient, but silly? Child-bearing. The great historic line of bleeding mothers, bleeding for humanity, for reproduction, for the future of the race. And this would go on for twenty or thirty years. How much blood would she lose? Would anyone notice? Would anyone give a damn?

Bleeding for mankind. The expression caught her attention. Wasn't that what Jesus had done? Were women Christian because they bled? What was this sacrifice? But Judy Kaplan did not appreciate these sentiments. Hers was a practical world, and she knew all about it because her father was a gynecologist. To her bleeding merely meant they were ready for a man, and Judy was always scheming about how to get together with the boys.

"Women bleed. Men give money," said Judy. "Did you know that they call the sperm money sometimes? They also call it blood. If a man comes, they call it giving blood. Or money. Isn't that funny?"

Judy eyed her, and then said, "Do you know what a checkbook Jew is?"

Then Judy, with all the might of her fourteen-year-old's information, explained to Rachel that giving was no real substitute for *aliyah*, or pilgrimage, observing the Sabbath, and keeping kosher. She told her that even the *United Jewish Fund* raised more money per year than the *American Heart*

Association, the *March of Dimes*, the *American Cancer Society*, the *Muscular Dystrophy Society*, and the *Easter Seal Society* combined. Then she read her a clipping from Daniel Eleazar saying that "organized activity — often philanthropic in character — has come to be the most common manifestation of Judaism, replacing prayer, study, and the normal private intercourse of kin as a source of being Jewish."

"Isn't that just fascinating?" said Judy. "You should know these things if you're a JAP."

"What's a JAP?" asked Rachel.

"A Jewish American Princess."

Actually, Rachel knew of this because checkbook Judaism did not bother Harry. *I give, therefore I am* made some sense to his existential nature, he had said. It was real. What irked him, he had told Deborah, was the organization of it, the group tactics. Rachel told Judy they had discussed it at the table and it made Harry mad to hear William Zuckerman say that American Jewry had almost consciously emptied itself of all higher aspirations and spiritual needs and had willingly limited itself to the role of financial milk cow for others. Zuckerman, Rachel remembered, asked how a community whose highest ideal is mechanical fund-raising could be the source of nobility and greatness. But for Harry, she remembered, the answer to that one was easy — by giving. Giving was, in his mind, a far harder and greater proof of reality than prayer.

"People say the Jews are trying to buy off guilt," said Judy.

"That's not the point for Harry," Rachel answered. "Would a kosher lunch save refugees? No. Would twenty thousand dollars? Yes. That's the difference, Harry says. It's a question of buying survival."

What Rachel didn't know was that Harry didn't want to become a vicarious Israeli, either. Somehow he had to steer a middle course between the schlemiels and the new image of super Jew. He abhorred the "Rambowitz" novels in which the hero is an Israeli who wears a silver chain under an open khaki shirt, bush shorts, and lug-soled hiking boots, while carrying in his hand a smoking Uzi automatic. Singing "Hatikvah," the Israeli anthem of hope, was one thing; looking at posters of a Hasid in a telephone booth taking off his long black coat to reveal a Superman costume was another.

"Harry is not your typical person who is outwardly American, inwardly a Jew," Rachel told Judy.

In fact, if anything, it was the other way around -outwardly a Jew, inwardly an American. If he had been pushed to admit it, Harry detested the siege mentality, and Rachel heard him complain of the endless statistics of the B'nai B'rith, showing that eighty percent of Americans distrust Jewish businessmen and that only three percent of them thought a Jew could be more honest than some other businessman. "All wrong," Harry said. Someone like Meir Kahane, who constantly predicted the worst for Jews in America, stirred Harry's wrath because Kahane fanned the very flames of bigotry that he said he opposed.

No, Harry was an armchair Jew. That is, his primary arena was not the pulpit, the synagogue, the B'nai B'rith, the activist committee, the Jewish Fund, but his head. An armchair does not mean inaction, nonparticipation, amorphousness, or passivity. It was simply that the theater of Judaism took place in his mind rather than in a show of piety or righteousness. For instance, he brooded over the fact that though six million Jews were exterminated (unsavory word, as if Kafka were loose) in Nazi ovens and executions, there lived almost six million Jews in the United States! The same number. Were they the same Jews, or echoes of each other? "It is hard to be a Jew." That was true even when, like Harry, one wasn't even really trying to be one.

Judy Kaplan nodded approval as Rachel explained her father.

"How much did they pay you for your Grandpa and Grandma?" asked Judy.

Rachel didn't know what she meant.

"Reparations," said Judy. "Everybody got money from the Germans for the relatives they killed."

"Nothing," said Rachel. "Grandpa and Grandma lived. They got away."

"You would be rich today," said Judy.

Rachel was shy. Somehow her first blood had opened this conversation and now she told Judy that it was funny, but there was a longing in part of her for the old orthodoxy, Sam's world, a high mehitzah, the barrier separating the women from the men. For not choosing your own husband even — it added to the mystery. Judy laughed. But Rachel said the men in skull caps and fur hats, the black suits, the prayer shawls — it all seemed like a world that the Hirsches, who were orthodox, had, and that Grandpa Sam remembered, but that had been taken away from them.

"Yes," Judy said, "Benny Hirsch is so funny. I could die teasing him. And he's never kissed a girl."

But it was colorful, Rachel said. The old ones, after all, despite the suffering, the exile, had enjoyed Jewishness. Their ethnicity, for all that it cut them off from the world, had also been fun. Harry didn't have that. What was there for Rachel instead — chewing gum, mini-skirts, pop music, cars, and T.V.? "A survivor has tested existence like the blade of a knife," said Rachel, "and they have a feel for the sharpness of life. They can remember even the dead in a tear. But we who are born today have no such identity. Harry says we have nothing but skepticism, superficiality, and secularism."

Judy giggled, and then repeated, "Pretty soon you'll need a diaphragm. Shall I call Asher and see if he'll come over and play with us?"

14   Sweet Sixteen

When Rachel was sixteen, the year she gave her first public concert, the trouble began, imperceptibly at first. It is always difficult to tell when a mental state begins; it is like a virus or a cold. The onset is almost imperceptible. Then it is there. She began to worry. Not full time, not even consciously — but just to worry. She would get wet palms, a little chill, anxiety. About what? Nothing. Or it seemed to be nothing. But secretly there was something. Something that nobody else would associate with nerves. Something that to everybody else was not a real problem, was, in fact, sort of a joke. If they thought about it at all. And they didn't. But Rachel began to. She began to worry that the Messiah would come.

The Messiah. Of all the things to worry about with AIDS at large, the ozone layer, the environment, the *intifadah*, Israel, Saddam Hussein, the breakup of Russia, the hydrogen bomb, crime in the streets, drugs, the economy, the starving children in Somalia, the "ethnic cleansing" in Bosnia, carbon in the air — with a hundred real disasters to worry about, not to mention her own school and her guitar career, who needed the Messiah to worry about? It wasn't even a real worry, was it? After all, for six thousand years or so, so far, he hadn't come, had he? What triggered Rachel to worry all of a sudden about the redeemer?

There is a saying in the Mid-East that every time they hear the call of the muezzin, the blare of prayer hours from the mosque turrets, that the Jews look out of their windows to see if the Messiah has come. It started to be that way for Rachel, even though there was no muezzin.

She couldn't identify when it began. Was it because her mother, Deborah, used to say, "Hurry up or you'll be late for the Messiah"? Or was it because the Jews were still waiting? In any case, it was the same year that she entered Brandeis University, with its three chapels that never cast a shadow on each other out in Waltham, Massachusetts, not far from Brookline.

Yet something sinister did cast a shadow on her. It was strange because it was not two thousand years of persecution that got to her, it was not the holocaust, it was not fear of another Jew burning, it was not the classic sense of Judaic guilt, it was not *angst* — it was an anxiety that she didn't even realize was affecting her because it was a question, it even seemed innocently to be an intellectual question. Not "When would the Messiah come?" but "What would they do to the Messiah when he did come?"

Maybe the thing that set it off was a clipping that her father showed her with a laugh. It was something that Menachem Begin, then the President of Israel, had said in Israel and that Harry thought was a good joke. Begin told some American Baptists visiting the Holy Land, "If you help us in the Congress, we'll help you at the Second Coming."

Ha! Ha! Harry thought it was sort of intriguing and amusing, but Rachel didn't laugh. She turned white.

The Christ, supposedly, had not come — not according to the Jews. So how could there be a *Second* Coming? What did President Begin mean?

It did not occur to Rachel that this was a joke. Nobody who had been a Jew over the last two thousand years could think that the promise of redemption was a joke. Belief in the Messiah was one of the cardinal points of belief of Judaism, one of the few basic principles — like Kashrut and the Sabbath. The food laws, like not cooking an egg on Saturday, or the law about not wearing wool mixed with cotton might be a joke. Harry could eat shrimp and make fun of it. But the Messiah? Redemption itself? The whole concept of the future betterment of man? The mission of the Jews?

That was not why Rachel turned white, however. Her sudden palidness came from something else, a misunderstanding, call it, because what Rachel thought Menachem Begin meant was that when the Second Coming came, the Jews would help the Baptists crucify Jesus. After all, that was what they had done the first time, wasn't it?

Rachel was only sixteen. She had never had a bar mitzvah. There were things she didn't understand. But she was a bright girl. She had a lot of questions. As to the crucifixion, she was under the impression — Jews really preferred not to talk about these things — that the Christians had crucified Christ. After all, they were Romans, weren't they? Jews didn't crucify people. They stoned them. But all the Romans were Catholics, and all the Catholics were Christians. Christianity was a Christian religion, right? The Jews didn't talk about it, and no one read the *New Testament*, which was where Christ was killed, so Rachel just assumed it was the Christians who killed him. That was why she never took it personally when the kids at school called the Jews "Christ killers." It didn't concern her. It was something the Christians had done.

Rachel had not studied theology yet, so she did not know she was confused. She had not read the gospels, so she didn't even really know the story. But now Menachem Begin said that the Jews would help the Christians at the Second Coming, which could only mean that the Jews would kill the Messiah, as the Christians had done the first time. This seemed like an awful idea, and if the Jews didn't kill the Messiah, then it stood to reason that the Christians would.

What Menachem Begin didn't understand was that children take the world seriously, and they take Redemption seriously. It means something to them, even if they don't understand all the details. The mission of the Jewish people, that is, to redeem the earth, was a real thing to Rachel. It was the reason she played the guitar. Christians thought the world was already saved because Jesus Christ had come. But the Jews couldn't let things be as they were. They couldn't accept the status quo. Precisely because the Messiah hadn't come yet. The world still needed to be saved. That much Rachel understood.

But the fate of the Messiah was another question. Rachel was just about to go to the university, and she didn't know all about the *Sadducees*, the *Zealots*, the *Essenes*, and the *Pharisees*, but she was bright enough to ask what if the Messiah had not yet come, what would happen to him when he did come? Not everybody is that bright, even if, like Menachem Begin, they think they know it all.

This question — what will actually happen when the Messiah does come — began to preoccupy Rachel. Some

Jews have thought about it, but Christians give it scarcely any thought. They should. There is going to be a lot of confusion when the Messiah does come, as Rachel vaguely feared, not only for Jews but especially for Christians. When the Jews finally do get around to having a Messiah, there is going to be a lot of soul-searching, not only among Jews but among Christians. People are going to ask, "Well, after all, has he really come before, or is this the first time? Is the Jewish Messiah the same as the Second Coming, or is he someone new? Does he come in a body, or does he come in a cloud — as the gospels say?"

These were all questions that secretly were gnawing at Rachel's young soul, even if Menachem Begin, the former president of Israel, the titular head of Zion, thought they were a crude political joke. Little children, however, are not crude. They do not understand that Menachem Begin could think of selling the Messiah for the support of the United States Congress. To children, the Messiah is a solemn thing. Religion is a reality. They have not yet learned to disbelieve.

Rachel was the same way. Naive, yes; crude, no. It would take Brandeis University to help her first to learn what belief is, and then to disbelieve it. We cannot cultivate disbelief without our universities, after all. But Rachel was not ready for this. The idea that the Jews might crucify the Messiah when he came began slowly to make her sick.

It was the beginning, in her world, of evil.

15   The Philosophy Class

The boy next to her in her freshman philosophy class was a redhead who kept nudging her arm. The lecture was on Spinoza. It was Professor Lenny Ratkin, who had a reputation for being unkosher — a liberal in wolf's clothing. He wore a turtleneck and a camel's-hair jacket to class. Rachel thought he was good-looking in a Jewish sort of way, with dark eyes that darted around the room. Only the jacket drooped on him, as if it had been hung in a closet too long, making him look as if he had been smoked like a salmon. He was known as the risque professor, who spoke openly in class about love and freedom and the Jews. He had started the semester with a joke about eggs — why do boiled eggs have a special significance for Jews? Because if they boil long enough they get hard. Ha! Ha!

But there was something haunted about Lenny Ratkin, as if some ghost of the ancestors were pursuing him, whispering over his shoulder. He used to cock an ear while lecturing, as if listening for the Meggid to inspire him from behind the blackboard. And he stood a little like a scarecrow, as if the camel's-hair jacket had been draped over him to scare off the voices of authority. Rachel was in awe of him. He had published a book called *The New Jew*, examining the philosophical source of Jewish-American thought, and Rachel immediately felt drawn to him. After all, she was only sixteen.

This was her first view of a truly liberated Jew. During class she floated in her seat with a warm feeling in her heart as Heraclitus, Plato, Aristotle, Moses, and the Prophets rolled by while Lenny related the connections between the modern mind and antiquity.

"If you don't stop nudging me, I'll tell the professor," Rachel finally said to the redhead.

"My name is Rick," he said. "You're the first friend I've made since matriculation. I've been watching you since opening day. Spinoza is wonderful, isn't he?"

Rachel looked at him. He was obviously Christian, a gentile. But Spinoza had caught all her attention, and she was tripped out on immanence. In fact, she had never known the difference before between immanence and transcendence —— somehow it clarified reality for her. After class she accepted Rick's invitation to go to the cafeteria.

"I just love *causa sui*, don't you?" said Rick. "It sounds like chop suey. Just think of God, the *ens necessarium*, being *causa sui*, the perfect primal ground of all reality, the one substance which is grounded in itself and through itself. Doesn't that make you just crawl?"

Rachel gave him a long-distance look that said no, but yes.

"I mean," said Rick, looking around. "I'm practically the only Christian around. Our God is supposed to be personal.

The Father and the Son are the same. He died on the cross just for us. Now someone called Baruch de Spinoza is telling me that God is the *natura naturans*, the ground of being — besides, I don't know any Jewish girls, so will you be my friend?"

He held out his hand.

Rachel burst out laughing.

"Why do you laugh?"

"Because I've never met a Christian boy before," she said.

"I'm not a boy. I'm nineteen," said Rick. "I took a year off before college."

"What did you do?"

"I worked as a dishwasher for six months. Then for six months I motorcycled around the country."

Her obvious question was why Rick had chosen Brandeis, but she didn't ask it.

Instead, Rick said, "I didn't get accepted at Harvard. My father was a New Dealer. He always admired Judge Brandeis. He told me to join "the juice." He said I'd get a broader, sharper education, and I'd learn something about people besides. He wants me to be a lawyer and thinks I can get into law school easier from Brandeis. If you can't beat them, you know, join them."

Although he was a redhead, Rick was extraordinarily good-looking. He had blue eyes and clear skin. No freckles.

"People say I look like Robert Redford," he said, embarrassed. "Do you think so?"

"No," said Rachel, lying.

"Good. I want to look like myself. Do you realize how hard it is to look like yourself? Particularly when you're young. Who do you look like?"

Rachel stared him in the eyes. "Myself."

"You're awfully young," said Rick. "How old are you? Sixteen? How did they let you loose in the den of lions?"

Rachel blushed. "I have my own maturity," she said. "Age doesn't matter."

Now Rick looked askance at her. "What do you think of Ratkin?" he asked.

For some reason she felt wary, as if the question were personal. She felt a twinge of shyness, as if she had been exposed. "The professor?" she said. "What would I want to do with the professor?"

"I don't know," he said, not aware of how prescient he was. "I thought you liked him. You seem not to be there when he talks."

It made her angry to be caught out. "If you want to know," she said, "I think Spinoza is the greatest philosopher that ever lived. He's the first really modern Jew."

"I prefer Pascal myself," said Rick, looking proud of himself.

"Pascal? Why?"

"Because he feels. He's not Cartesian. I think feeling is important," said Rick.

Rachel hadn't thought of it. "Pascal isn't modern," she said.

"Oh, he is. He connects to the existentialists. Subjectivity. Intensity. Passion." Rick looked happy.

Rachel felt slightly deflated. "Immanence" had been such a big new word for her, but she looked at Rick with new respect.

"The existentialists?" she said.

Rick looked pleased with himself. But something else was happening. He looked into Rachel's flecked brown eyes and began to fall in love. But it was like a philosopher falling in love. Or a Christian. And he gazed at her knowing that there was some connection between them, but that it somehow meant trouble. Affliction.

"What's your name?" Rick asked after a pause.

Rachel hesitated. For a moment she wanted to say Rose, or Joan, or Harriet. She didn't know why. Was it because Rachel was Jewish or because she didn't want to give herself away? She also perceived that Rick had some special kind of authority over her because he was good-looking or because he was older or for some other reason that she could not figure out.

"Rachel," she said, and she suddenly thought nonsensically that it would have been funny if his name were Jacob. But of all the boys in the class, he was the least likely.

"Rachel."

"Laban's daughter," said Rick. "'Leah was tender-eyed, but Rachel was well-favored and beautiful.'"

"I thought Christians only read the New Testament," said Rachel.

"I went to Bible school," said Rick. "Rachel… So Rachel, who is Rachel really?"

Rachel thought for a moment. "Well, she said, "I'm a guitarist."

"That's wonderful," Rick said. "I play the bass." And he drummed his fingers on the table.

"That's a coincidence," said Rachel.

"A coincidence?" Rick repeated. "Spinoza did not allow for anything indeterminate in the world. As Einstein said, 'The Old One does not play dice.' Rachel, I think we met in heaven."

"This is heaven?" said Rachel sarcastically, looking around.

"No," said Rick, "but do you mind if I admit something to you?"

"What?"
"You're beautiful," Rick said, and it was the first time Rachel had heard it from anyone but the mirror.

16   The Blue Cafe

The Blue Guitar Cafe was tucked into the back of a Massachusetts Avenue storefront between Harvard and M.I.T. It had checked oil cloth table doilies, round tables with wire-backed chairs, a seedy portico and stage up front, and ramshackle service with avocado sandwiches. You could get drinks and soup. A little poster in black and white advertised the Mango and Chile Quartet, with Rick Lauron on bass.

Rachel sipped a lemonade. The music seemed like the unfinished business of the world, a mixture of Latin and rock, but it wasn't as cerebral, as hopeless as modern jazz, where no resolution ever seemed to pave the way to a future and where the present riffed like an inextricable tangle that could never get away from itself. Modernity. An idea with no place to go. She argued with Rick about it. He was less fatalistic than she, but at least they both agreed that the Latin rock had feeling and could come up against a climax, could paint the moon against a starry night, could resolve the pangs of love. Rick said that modern jazz was a kind of purist philosophy — technicalities of music that referred the note to itself and should not be judged by mood, by lyricism, by the painted backdrop of a theater that wasn't there. It didn't have a reference, like Latin. But to Rachel this wasn't a substitute for classicism and the frenetic jazz was like futility sending messages to itself, whereas Latin rock was at least a melody tripping somewhere on a rhythm.

They played the first set with Rick on the bass. Then he came over to her table. It had been Bossa Nova. He sat down lightly and ordered a glass of wine. The young people were a mixture of college eccentrics and nonschool X-ers and other locals. The waitress was out of a movie in which the casting director had rejected her for the role, and the storyline was of some broken love that lay in pieces like shattered glass on the floor.

Neither of them smoked.

"Nothing is more difficult than to become the person you have always claimed to be," said Rick for an opener.

"If we were meant to be ourselves," said Rachel.

"Of course we were."

"That's easy for you to say. But you were never consigned to an oven."

Rick drummed his fingers. "So what saved me?"

"Christianity."

He had never thought of it that way. Salvation was a theological concept. It had never come down to death and life, and he grinned. "So something I never chose saved me from the cattle cars," he said.

"If you like," she responded. "Something that chose me might have marked me for Zyklon B. It's something to think about. Are we free? I mean free at all."

Tyler, the lead guitarist, joined them. He was blond, blue-eyed. He told Rachel he was glad to meet her and ordered a beer.

"Love," said Rick.

"Love what?" Rachel asked.

"Love is freedom," Rick answered.

"That's cool. That's really cool," said Tyler.

Neither of them responded.

"I mean, really cool. You should found a political party."

"Well," said Rick defensively, "neither capitalism nor communism are free. Religion is bondage. So what is there?"

Tyler looked at him sadly. "Love, my friend, is a sickness."

Rick looked at Rachel. She was a picture of desire, an advertisement that promoted no product. She was youth as an end unto itself, beauty as the portrait of an unknown artist. She had nothing to sell. There was no price tag on her. She didn't come packaged yet with her past. Her name was not experience.

"The name of love is a slavery that deludes the soul," said Tyler.

Rick shook his head. "And you say you're a musician."

Tyler tightened. "What's it got to do with music?"

Rick leaned toward him. "The shape of it, man. Melody is love."

Rachel brightened. "I thought we were talking about the holocaust."

"That's it," Tyler said. "Love is a holocaust."

Rachel looked at him soberly. "The holocaust was sickness. Everybody whom it has touched receives an emotional intensity that derives from its basis in fact. It helps distinguish the actual from the unreal. Love is like anything we feel after the final solution."

Tyler gulped. "I didn't mean to get personal," he said.

"Be glad," Rick said, "that there are some illusions. A world without desire to even mislead us would be as dead as the real moon. Would you even be playing with Mango and Chile if there were no love? Be grateful for small things."

That seemed to end the conversation but not the subject — the subject seemed only to have begun. Like a book. Rachel was the first page of a new novel. Rick felt as if he had never read anything like it before. Tyler could go to hell.

It was time for a new set. Rick helped Rachel up on stage and introduced her as a guest artist of the Blue Guitar who "played things as they really are." Rachel took a little bow and opened her carrying case to fish out a classical guitar, which she had painted blue. The crowd applauded.

Then she sat on the stool in front of the mike and launched into *Sociagadamente* and *Desafinado*, which she and Rick had practiced together. The magic of the evening started anew as the soft notes spilled sidewise into the cafe and captured the illusion of imagined love.

Afterwards they returned to the round table with checkered oil cloth doilies and sat slightly exhausted, looking at each other.

"Melody is not entirely free. It's always somewhat predetermined," said Rick.

"I know what you mean," Rachel responded.

Rick took her hand. "I don't mean to intrude," he said, "but, Rachel, you've got this thing for Ratkin. You may not even know it. But be careful, Rachel. Be careful of the professor."

17   The Lecture

The night of the lecture was rainy. It was on the Historicity of Jesus, a suitably postmodern theme, but Rachel thought, if she knew Lenny Ratkin, that he would have something up his sleeve. Though Jesus was such a famous character, no one really talked much about him, not Jews at least. She wondered what Lenny -of all people — could say. After all, faith aside, Jesus either existed or he didn't. What Rachel secretly wanted to know was not about historicity but his personality — who was he? In fact, was he the Messiah? That would have been her lecture. She was going expectantly, along with Rick, who was rather put off by the title.

"I mean," said Rick, "Jesus is a belief. We don't ask if he was historical. History really doesn't have to do with faith. Besides, we hear about the Christ rather than Jesus. Christ wasn't a person in the historical sense. He was divine. Jesus must have been a person, not in the sense of the Trinity, but a person person. Somehow. I'm surprised the subject is on Ratkin's short list, however."

"Lenny is a person, too," said Rachel as they slid into seats in the auditorium.

"You should know," said Rick.

"What does that mean?"

"You're the one who likes him."

Rachel blushed despite herself. She had no answer.

"At least he's a good professor," Rick said as Lenny shuffled in. Lenny was wearing a turtleneck sweater and tweed coat. He looked as if he had been up all night. He fumbled around at the podium. Gradually the hall fell silent. There were at least two hundred people present, and it was a mixed audience. Some of the crowd were older.

"There is a joke among Jews," Ratkin began. "It goes, 'Yes, we killed him. We killed him because he didn't want to be a doctor.' The comedian might have added, 'Or a lawyer.' The joke would then be complete. But there is some history behind this joke, and that's what we want to get at today."

Lenny came around to the front of the podium. "You notice the joke uses the collective 'we.' Well, just for the record, 'Non culpa mea.' Look, I believe in the Golden Rule and the Ten Commandments, and that puts me pretty close to a Christian."

He went back to the podium. "For two thousand years, since St. Paul — a Jew, incidentally, who began his career by persecuting Christians — Jews have been reviled and persecuted as 'Christ killers.' Deicides. People who kill God. St. Paul and St. John and the Greeks may have started it, or their followers. But Paul, or Saul, started the other way around. It says in *Acts, Chapter 8, Verse 3,* 'But Saul laid waste the church and entering house after house, he dragged off men and women and committed them to prison.'

"This is the man to whom St. Paul's Basilica in Rome is dedicated, and St. Paul's Cathedral in London. It makes you think about the whims of history."

Professor Ratkin paused and looked over his audience. Eighty percent of them were Jewish.

"The truth is that excommunication of Christians by Jews preceded the persecution of Jews by Christians. Early on, it was the powerful synagogues that repudiated the small Christian community as an apocalyptic messianic sect so that the Jews, by turning on Christians, by stoning Stephen, by codifying the oral Torah into the Talmud, created anti-Christianism. This is one of the great ironies of history. As early as Rabbi Gamaliel II (about 90 to 100 A.D.), and the council of Jabneh, curses against the apostates were inserted into the benedictions to be said three times a day. 'For the apostates let there be no hope. And let the arrogant government be speedily uprooted in our days. Let the Nazarenes (*nossim*) and the heretics (*minim*) be destroyed in a moment. And let them be blotted out of the Book of Life and not be inscribed together with the righteous. Blessed art thou, O Lord, who humbles the arrogant.'

"People forget this. Nicodemus the Pharisee visits Jesus by night. Why? Even Joseph of Arimathea remained only a secret disciple of Jesus for 'fear of the Jews.' In effect, very early on, the Jews threw the Jewish Christians out of the synagogue, and this had social and economic consequences."

Lenny was hitting his stride, but Rachel wondered if this was what she had come for. The audience, somewhat startled by the revelation about Jewish prejudice, was all attention.

"The wheel turned. And for two thousand years the Jews were reviled, persecuted, discriminated against, exiled, killed, and burned — sometimes by no less an institution, a

Christian institution and authority, than the Catholic Church.

"It was only in 1964 that the Vatican at the Twenty-Second Ecumenical Council, got around to officially condemning the view that Jews should be made scapegoats for the killing of Christ. This document was *NOSTRA AETATE*, an official council decree, which said, 'What happened in Jesus' passion cannot be blamed upon all the Jews then living, without distinction, nor upon the Jews of today.'

"But what of history"?

"What are we to make of the record that says, 'Then all the people cried out before Pilate, 'His blood be on us and on our children.' *Matthew 27:25?*

"Who, historically, was this personage at the center of this terrible and long controversy? Was he, in fact, historical?

"Or is the whole story of Jesus a *theologoumenon* — a theological insight narrated and dressed up as an historical event. Is it true or false?

"One scholar has said, 'There is no neutral Switzerland of the mind in the world of Jesus research.' Not only that. But even at its best, this quest can reconstruct only fragments of a mosaic, the faint outline of a faded fresco that allows many interpretations.

"The trouble is, there are at least three Jesuses: The Jesus of history; the real Jesus; and the Jesus of faith.

"Perhaps we should mention two more, the earthly Jesus, Jesus the Nazarene; and the heavenly Jesus, the Jesus called Christ.

"First of all, Jesus was a Jew." At this Lenny looked around the audience for affirmation. Rachel's interest stirred. "This will come as a surprise to many Jews, who think of Jesus as a Christian. It means, for one thing, that Jesus was a monotheist. He believed in the one true God.

"So why are there still Jews today who spit when the name of Jesus is mentioned? Martin Buber called him 'Great Brother.' And Jews reject Jesus as the second person of the Trinity, the Son, precisely because he was a Jew. Judaism can have only one god.

"But Jesus, as a Jew, would have rejected this Trinity, too. Already we are dealing with the difference between the historical Jesus, the real Jesus, and the Jesus of Faith. Jesus is supposed to have said, 'Why do you call me good? No one is good but God alone.' The Trinity is a confusing conceptual game involving three *hypostases*, persons, or *prosopa*, two processions and four relations, plus a distinction between nature and person. This seems absurd and blasphemous to Jews both of today and yesterday. These are all Greek categories. Is it really believable that Jesus, with all his earthy Jewishness, would have accepted the Hellenistic definition of himself as being 'of the same substance as God?'

"In fact, he referred to himself as the Son of Man, according to the Bible. This term had a Jewish history. It is never Jesus himself that claims to be the Son of God, although he uses the word 'Father' for God. But this, too, has Old Testament origins, as in *Samuel 7; 12-14*: 'I will raise up your seed after you... and I shall establish his kingly rule... and I shall make firm his throne forever. I will be his father and he shall be my son.'

"This story of Jesus is a Jewish history. Thus, Christians, too, are surprised to hear that Jesus was a Jew. They had always thought of him as a Christian. This slowly gets us to the difference between the Jesus of faith and the historical Jesus.

"What is there to say? Very little about the actual history, a lot about the history of the history. For instance, it is a fact of history, disputed by almost no scholar, that shortly after the death of Jesus some Jews, including people who had been his closest followers (all Jews, incidentally) during his public ministry, gathered to revere and celebrate him as the Messiah and Lord, to recall and hand on his teachings and to spread his teaching among other Jews.

"On the other hand, Jesus makes scarcely any impression on first century Jewish or other chronicles (Josephus and Tacitus) — he was insignificant to chronicle in the national and world history of Jews and pagans in the first century. The main historical data, curiously enough, seem to confirm that he died.

"The New Testament writings are not documentary reports nor neutral scientific historiography. They are, on the whole, committed testimonies of faith. They document the Jesus of Faith or, in part, the real Jesus. Mostly they refer to the years of the public ministry. There is scarcely anything about the childhood years or the so-called 'lost' years before Jesus was thirty.

"However, the *Quest for the Historical Jesus*, as Albert Schweitzer titled his book, still continues, and Karl Barth, Rudolf Bultmann, Paul Tillich, and the Jew Samuel Sandmel, among others, have sought the historical record. They take the testimonies of the gospels not to be simply reports but to have their foundations in reports of the real Jesus. Recently there have been scores of books on the subject.

"But even before we ask who Jesus was, we have to ask, historically, if he existed at all.

"The answer is yes.

"Even Samuel Sandmel, the Jewish scholar, maintains that certain bare facts are 'historically not be be doubted.' But what is known can be put by him into one paragraph. 'Jesus, who emerged into public notice in Galilee when Herod Antipas was its Tetrarch, was a real person, the leader of a movement. He had followers, called disciples. The claim was made, either by or for him, that he was the long-awaited Jewish Messiah. He journeyed from Galilee to Jerusalem, possibly in 29 or 30, and there he was executed, crucified by the Romans as a political rebel. After his death, his disciples believed that he was resurrected, and had gone to heaven, but would return to earth at the appointed time for the final divine judgement of mankind.'

"Let us compare this with the only authoritative non-canonical witness to Jesus' life from antiquity, the so-called *Testimonium Flavianium*, which appears in *Jewish Antiquities*, written around 93-94 by Joseph ben Mathias, a Jewish aristocrat, politician, soldier, turncoat, and historian.

"His passage reads: 'At this time there appeared Jesus, a wise man, if indeed one should call him a man. For he was a doer of startling deeds, a teacher of people who receive the truth with pleasure. And he gained a following both among many Jews and among many of Greek origin. He was the Messiah. And when Pilate, because of an accusation made by the leading men among us, condemned him to the cross, those who had loved him previously did not cease to do so. For he appeared to them on the third day, living again, just as the divine prophets had spoken of these and countless other wondrous things about him. And up until this very day the tribe of Christians, named after him, has not died out.'"

Lenny coughed.

"Parts of this statement are contested by historians as not being original, but it is the only known passage we have outside the Bible except for Tacitus. Unfortunately, Tacitus's *Annals* are not complete. His record for the years 29 A.D. through 31 A.D. are lost from the manuscript. So, unless a fuller manuscript is found, we will never know whether Tacitus mentioned Jesus in his treatment of the years 30-31. Tacitus does mention Jesus elsewhere, however, in reference to the great fire of Rome, for which Nero was himself suspected. 'Therefore,' says Tacitus, 'to squelch the rumor, Nero created scapegoats and subjected to the most refined tortures those whom the common people called *Christians*, hated for their abominable crimes. Their name comes from Christ, who, during the reign of Tiberius, had been executed by the prosecutor Pontius Pilate.'

"Again we have an authoritative citation of Christ's death — the best known fact about him. In fact, the whole debate between Jews and Christians about Jesus hinges on the last two days of Jesus' thirty-three years — Good Friday to Sunday.

"But a few other supposed facts have a broad Jewish-Christian consensus as historical findings: that Jesus came from Nazareth of Galilee; that he was born the son of the carpenter Joseph and Miriam; that he grew up with several brothers and sisters; that he had himself been baptized by John; that as an itinerant preacher he announced the kingdom of God and urged repentance; that he was reputed to perform healings; that he broke with his family and gathered disciples; that he found a hearing among the poor, the outcast, the sick, and women; that he got into an embroilment with Jewish authorities; that he finally met a violent death.

"The question arises: Why was Christianity not a Jewish religion? Jewish, but different. Certainly Jesus was a monotheist; certainly he belonged in the bosom of Abraham; certainly he was out to fulfill, not break, the law. Why, then, was the Jesus' movement not simply a Jewish reform movement?"

At this Lenny looked around the room. To Rachel it seemed like a good question, one she had not thought of, but she wondered how many of the Jews in the room would like to be reformed, even now. Rick nudged her.

"We know Jesus' history not by the record itself but by the history, too, of his surroundings. And we know that there were four prominent types of Jews in Jesus' day: the Sadducees, who were keepers of the temple and the power elite; the zealots, who were revolutionaries; the *Quumran, Essene,* and ascetic people, who were for emigration and withdrawal from society; and the Pharisees, who were upholders, observers of the law in practice.

"Jesus was not a zealot. He did not preach outward revolution or violence against Caesar. He was not withdrawn, not a monk, not an ascetic, though he appears to have had contacts with the *Essenes.* He is often contrasted with the Pharisees, who outwardly observed custom and law and are also pictured as hypocrites in the Bible. Jesus in some ways was closest to one of the seven types of Pharisee, the so-called love Pharisee. These people wanted to take God's commandments seriously but also make the law tolerable in everyday life.

"Finally, and most importantly, Jesus was not a Sadducee — he was not a priest, doctor, or lawyer, nor a keeper of the temple, and he did not belong to the Jewish power elite.

"But now we are asking ourselves who Jesus really was — not the historical Jesus but the real Jesus. Historically he existed. This is a fact. It is fundamental. But we have established most of the facts that can be spoken for him. It remains, from the history of society around him, to draw the suppositions together which paint a picture of the real man.

"This picture is <u>not</u> of a man who conforms to society. He is a layman, from common people, an itinerant, evidently unmarried, not an ascetic monk, one who did not live in exclusion from the world, who made contact with the disreputable, with those who, according to the Pharisees, were 'unclean.' Purity of heart was for him more important than any regulations of righteousness."

At this, Lenny looked at the audience directly and said, in an aside, "How many of us can say the same thing about ourselves?" He coughed again and went on.

"He did not preach class divisions or religious divisions — sons of light, sons of darkness. Forgiveness was free to all who repented. He was not a zealot for revolution or for the law. He did not stipulate abstinence. He ate and drank with his followers. He did not preach against marriage. He did not impose celibacy, or even renunciation of material goods. He lay down no religious rule. There was no novitiate, no entrance oath, no vow. He did not call for regular pious practices or long prayers, ritual meals or baths, or distinctive cloths.

"He did not establish an interminable liturgy, but called for a constant attitude of prayer on the part of those who expect everything from God all the time.

"His program was the *Sermon on the Mount*. He preached love of enemies, to forgive rather than to strike back, to be ready to suffer rather than use force, to bless the peacemakers rather than sing songs of hate and revenge. He spoke of a kingdom of Heaven. Those who live by the sword shall perish by the sword. Render unto Caesar what is Caesar's, and unto God what is God's.

"He got embroiled in the temple cleansing — but he did not occupy the temple; instead, he exercised a prophetic provocation against marketing and profiteering in a place of prayers.

"And, finally, when arrested, he was unarmed.

"What we have here is a picture of a man outside convention, a marginal man, an outsider, who is strange, unusual, ambiguous, perhaps unstable, perhaps subversive, impoverished, substandard, jobless, migrant, in transition, deviant, and nonconformist. Yet somehow noble.

"Thus, we come to his death. More than many men, Jesus is defined by his death.

"There appears to have been some kind of trial on Thursday night by a committee of Sadducees belonging to the Sanhedrin. Much is uncertain about this. It may have been an interrogation. They may or may not have passed a sentence. It appears unlikely that the direct, formal question whether Jesus was the Messiah or son of God was an accusation. Besides, the Jews did not possess the *ires gladii*, the legal power of execution. So they turned the results of their interrogation over to the Romans, Pontius Pilate, the prefect.

"But the kinds of charges that may have been leveled against Jesus stand clear from the gospels as a whole. Jesus was a seemingly radical critic of the traditional religious practices of many law-abiding Jews. Jesus had protested and prophesied against the Temple. Jesus held human beings more important than the law. His association with outcasts was scandalous. He was critical of ruling groups.

"In a word, he was the first modern, existential, common man — a precursor of our contemporary man, who decides his own life on the basis of conscience.

"But the Jews turned him over to Pilate, procurator of Judea (26-36 A.D.), and in accordance with Roman custom, the inscription on the cross records the particular grounds for condemnation (*causa damnationis*). 'King of the Jews' could only be understood in political terms by the Romans. The claim to a royal title was an infringement of Roman majesty (*crimen laesae maiertatis*).

"It was a false charge. 'King of the Jews' was not even synonymous with 'Messiah.' A charge of political treason was a trumped-up charge — Jesus did not even call on people to refuse taxes. So when the trial went before Pilate, there was a miscarriage of justice — and justice was the first of the Roman rights!

"The religious charge behind the political one could only have had to do with Jesus' critical attitude to the law and the Temple — an offence that amounted to a religious misdemeanor. But, as Martin Buber said, it was Jesus' 'exaggerated Judaism' that was to blame for his situation — he was the Jewish reformer *par excellence* of Jewish institutions.

"Yet it is the Romans who were to blame for his death. In two thousand years the Jews have been called deicides, while the Romans, who mischarged and misjudged and put him to death, have built the Holy Roman Catholic Church on the remains of the empire that killed Christ. No one has called them God killers.

"But it was this death which at the time defined the life. The cross was the equivalent of the electric chair. This was the death of a common criminal. It made his death terrifying and disgusting. His death, the form of it, made Jesus himself offensive. This was before all the pretty pictures of the crucifixion.

"The one hanged on a tree is the accursed of God.

"The horror of this death cannot be stressed enough. It was the lowliest, most ignoble, most disgusting of deaths that could be suffered. There was no glory in it, anymore than there is glory in death row, the gas chamber, or the electric chair, Less, even.

"Thus, we come to the irony of the Jews. We are not going to speak of the Jesus of Faith. That is another subject. Our concern is Jesus, the historical Jew. Not the God of the Christians. As Pinchas Lapide said, 'That God needs a human sacrifice to reconcile his own creation with himself, that he, the ruler of the world, cannot justify anyone without a blood sacrifice is as incomprehensible to Jews as it is contrary to the Bible.'

"Yet Max Nordau, collaborator of Theodor Herzl, the father of Zionism, said, 'Jesus is the soul of our soul, as he is the flesh of our flesh. So who can exclude him from the Jewish People?'

"This is the great karma of irony of the Jews, that Jesus, rejected in his mission to the Jews themselves, his new Jewish religion rejected, still appears, in an entirely civil perspective, as the primal figure of the Jewish people, persecuted in the world and condemned to unspeakable sorrow.

"Seeing Jesus as a Jew, an earthman from Nazareth, although it makes him more accessible than the Son of God, nevertheless makes it even harder on Jews because he is not

God. For Christians, in contrast, it is easy: He overcomes. But for the Jews, Jesus becomes an existential man whose history is even harder to explain and bear on historical terms than it is on divine terms. In some ways, this is the Jewish way — there is no excuse nor triumph for Jesus because of divinity. The grounds of his story, his existence, his passion, death, and, yes, even resurrection — resurrection, contrary to belief, is an article of Jewish faith — have to be found in his existential grounds as a man. A Jewish man.

"He is the teacher, yet rejected; he is the prophet, yet misunderstood; he is the witness, yet betrayed; he is the judge, yet judged; he is the high priest himself, yet he is sacrificed; finally, as the king, he is crowned with thorns, and as the victor, crucified.

"No Jewish history is complete without humor. There is the story of the circus lion in Warsaw whom an unemployed Jew is hired to kill in the show. As he stabs the lion, he recites the Jewish prayers for the dead — and the lion responds in yiddish. The lion recites all the proper responses. 'What is going on?' the Jew asks, and the lion answer, 'You are not the only Jew in Poland looking for a job.'

"But Jesus, if I may suggest it, is the greatest Jewish joke there is."

At this Rachel gasped, and, clutching Rich, she whispered, "He's going to spoil it all."

"And he is a joke perpetrated on the Jews by themselves. He is the joke of the Davidic line. Christian expectation of the Messiah severed the polarity of the traditional Jewish title of Messiah and the traditional expectations — it had meant the plenipotentiary and bringer of revelation, the Son of Man, Messiah of God; it denoted the mighty warrior hero of the end of time and royal liberator of peoples. But, suddenly, in Jesus, 'King of the Jews,' it denoted a nonviolent, defenseless, misunderstood, betrayed, and finally suffering and dying Messiah — and this view, this fate, this joke was played by Jews upon themselves. He was the archetypal suffering Jew — and the Jews rejected him."

Lenny paused. He drew a breath and said slowly, "As a result, Jesus became the most famous Jew of them all.

"In conclusion, two thoughts. One, from the Torah, the Jews own argument: namely, only God can forgive guilt, only the victims can forgive. Thus, the living have to live with guilt.

"The other question is: 'Was Jesus the Messiah?'" Here Rachel involuntarily leaned forward in her chair.

"And this is where we shall end for today, with a quote from Franz Rosenzweig: 'Whether Jesus was the Messiah will become evident for the Jews when the Messiah comes.' Thank you."

Lenny walked off. There was a silence and some shuffling in the audience before the applause.

18 The Benefit

Rachel had never stayed at a place like the Waldorf Astoria before, with its big canopied entryway, the carpeted reception hall, the chandeliers, the marble, the uniformed livery. The palatial stairways were something out of a movie.

Her room was a quaint, old-fashioned room, with the covers turned back, its own telephone and refrigerator, and prints of ducks on the walls. She didn't belong here. The furniture was antique and the windows looked out onto grand old New York.

She set her guitar case down in the corner and thought it over. All expenses paid, and a fee! She wondered how Horowitz and Rubinstein and Isaac Stern had felt before concerts, what they did in the afternoon. She thought of Andres Segovia coming to town with his guitar — a wooden guitar against all of this city — and whether anybody would be able to hear her in all this traffic. Segovia had said, "A performance is like raising Lazarus. The work lies dead in the tomb. The performer comes along and says, 'Arise and walk.'"

She hoped she would be up to it. She lay down and tested the bed. A little nap. The light fell softly through soft white curtains, and she dreamed. She dreamed the Messiah came to her concert at Carnegie Hall, but nobody recognized him. He was dressed British but spoke Yiddish. He was young. He sat in row H, on the aisle, and he was with a young girl. He was good-looking, but he might have been anyone. The police were looking for him, but he wasn't concerned.

Then a bunch of officials broke into the concert, marched down the aisles, and took him into custody. There were some hoodlums with them, and they brought the Messiah up onstage and shoved Rachel and her guitar off. Then in the spotlight, they crucified him. Music seemed to be everywhere. The orchestra was playing Mozart. Before he died on the cross, he looked up at the audience and said, "Where is Rachel?"

She woke up.

Her first thought was how big the city was and how small a girl she was. She thought of what Segovia had said: "I was my own teacher and student, and due to the mutual effort of both, they were not displeased with each other." Then she thought of Segovia's first concert when on the way to the concert hall an old flutist stopped him on the street and asked, "Do you know this guitarist?" "Yes, very well," said Segovia. "Is he talented?" asked the flutist. "Not at all," said Segovia. The flutist showed up at the concert and afterwards came up to Segovia and embraced him. "You are lucky to be this fellow's friend," said the flutist, "and you are right to be jealous of him." Rachel wondered if anything like that would happen to her.

Her manager called — Walt Levine. He was downstairs. "I'll take you to the benefit," he said.

It was the benefit for the Jewish Emergency Fund, a late afternoon affair in the Waldorf Astoria ballroom. Rachel dressed for her concert, a new green evening gown with a black shawl. She wasn't sure that green was the right color, but the dress clung around her thighs. She wore green high heel shoes and had a Spanish comb in her auburn hair.

"You look fine," said Walt downstairs, and he escorted her to the ballroom. "This will keep you from getting nervous."

Everybody seemed to be on the guest list except Maimonides, Isaiah, the Rosenbergs, and Caiaphas. It read like a *Who's Who of America*. Rachel cast a glancing eye over it and caught some of the names: Isaac Bashevis Singer, Henry Kissinger, Arthur Goldberg, Norman Mailer, Irwin Shaw, Nathan Birnbaum (George Burns), Julius Garfinkel (John Garfield), Marion Levy (Paulette Goddard), Betty Perske (Lauren Bacall), Bess Myerson, Ed Koch, Hank Greenberg, Bernard Malamud, Philip Roth, Chaim Potok, Mark Harris, Leon Uris, Sandy Koufax, Rabbi Alexander Goode, Laura Z. Hobson, Norman Podhoretz, Irving Howe, Horowitz, Rubinstein, Barry Goldwater, Arthur Murray, Abby and Ann Landers, Ralph Lauren, Alfred Kazin, Lionel Trilling, Lee Strasberg, Susan Strasberg, Irving Berlin, Irving Saypol, Irving R. Kaufman, Walter Annenberg, Harold T. Shapiro, Irving Shapiro, Edward H. Levi, Neil L. Rudenstine, Eugene V. Rostow, Arthur Schlesinger, Eddie Fisher, Arthur Miller, Woody Allen, Daniel Boorstin, Richard Hofstadter, Walter Lippmann, David Broder, Joseph Kraft, Anthony Lewis, Herbert Marcuse, Julius Rosenwald, Louis B. Mayer, Gerard Swope, Ivan Boesky, Michael Milliken, David Sarnoff, Alec Flamm, Henry Kravis, Felix Rohatyn, Leonard

Stern, Warren Phillips, Stephen Spielberg's mother, Red Buttons, Danny Kaye, Jerry Lewis, Milton Berle, Mort Sahl, William L. Levitt, Whoopi Goldberg, Abbie Hoffman, Sammy Davis, Jr., Lynda Carter, Betty Friedan, Dhalamith Firestone, Susan Brownmiller, Andrea Dworkin, and Robin Morgan. Even Marilyn Monroe and Elizabeth Taylor were on the short list.

Who said a Jew couldn't make it in America?

But the people Rachel most wanted to meet were characters like Rabbi Small, Len Cantrow, Allan Felix and Linda Christie, Kosher Kitty Kelly, Abie, the Cohens, and Robert Cohn.

Marjorie Morningstar was there.   Correction: Marjorie Morgenstern.   Correction again: Mrs. Milton Schwartz. Rachel couldn't believe her eyes or, rather, her ears. She was remarkably gray, and her face had wizened, but she was still attractive. She wasn't slim anymore, rather matronly, yet she had a presence that wouldn't go away despite age. Somehow, somewhere, she was still on stage. Her children, grown up, were with her, and a portly, authoritative, stubby sort of man was near her who must be Milton Schwartz, the lawyer.

Rachel stared at her, wondering what would become of herself with time — what troubled her, she guessed, was the thought of the bright vision that had faded. To Rachel, too, she was really Marjorie Morningstar. And if she wasn't the bright angel that Wally Wronken thought, that Noel Airman baited, she had been a lovely girl — and where was that girl now? Was Rachel's concert the same illusion in the glitter and traffic of New York? Would she not even remember herself as she was in a few years?

It was the same atmosphere Rachel was suddenly in at the Waldorf Astoria that it must have been decades ago — only the century was over, it wore its scars, the millennium was come. Otherwise, the champagne was similar. There were still the greedy, hot, stuffed hors d'oeuvres, the imported salmon, the rare roast beef, the flaming cherries jubilee. Noel Airman, old and bald, came by, and Wally Wronken, the playwright, stood next to Marjorie. It was like having stars in one's eyes.

Her manager introduced her. "Mrs. Schwartz, this is Rachel Rosevale, the guitarist."

"Oh, my," said Marjorie. Some kind of familiarity seized the older woman. "We should talk, dear, but this is impossible."

Rachel nodded. "It's such a privilege to meet you," she said. "I'm a believer in Marjorie Morningstar."

Marjorie laughed pleasantly. She had aplomb, and she still had the contralto voice. For a moment, a flash of brilliance touched her matron's blue eyes, and she said, "You are the star I never was."

Rachel blushed. "Did you read Herman Wouk's book about you? What did you think?" Looking around at the sophisticated crowd in evening dress and gowns, Rachel felt embarrassed at asking such a childish question.

But Marjorie smiled warmly. "In many ways it was not a deep book," she said sharply but not unkindly. "How could it be? It was an everyday, mundane book, you know. Marjorie Morningstar aspired to the lights, to glitter, to fame. But, actually, Wouk's is a humble story. It must seem old-fashioned stuff to you today, but there was one part at the end that made me think."

"Wally Wronken's diary."

"Yes. Where he says, 'And where is that girl now?' For the life of me, Rachel, I don't know. Are you her?"

"No," Rachel said, laughing. "I am a book of my own, if you only knew. But I loved the parts about New York, the view out from the El Dorado, the taxi cabs, the bars, the restaurants, the hotels, even the lilacs in the spring."

"Yes, they were lovely." At this moment Milton Schwartz approached. Rachel wanted to ask if, with age, a little love for Noel Airman had not returned somehow to flutter around her older heart, but it was too late.

"I see Portnoy is here," said Schwartz. "What kind of party is this, anyway?" And there's Asher Lev, the painter. And Barbara Streisand. It's all too much for an old man."

"You're not old, Milton. This is Rachel Rosevale, the guitarist. She has a concert in New York."

Schwartz looked at her. "Be careful of Portnoy," he said. "He eats sweet girls like you. My. You remind me of Marjorie. How many years ago is it now?"

"She's much prettier," said Marjorie, to be kind.

But Schwartz said, "No. Not prettier. More beautiful, maybe. But not prettier."

Marjorie gave her husband a kiss. Rachel said, "Actually, Marjorie and I are very different."

"Well, I'm glad to hear it. I don't know why. But it must be so. The times are very different. Harsher, I'd say. But more bountiful, too. We lost our innocence in the Second World War. But I daresay nowadays youth isn't even born innocent."

Rachel wanted to say something more to Marjorie, but she couldn't think of how to bridge their generations. Most of all, she wanted to ask Marjorie Morningstar, Mrs. Schwartz, if she was, well — waiting for the Messiah? Mike Eden had asked her in the boat on the lake in Lucerne, when he was telling about rescuing the kids from Germany, "In case you have any lingering doubts that I'm stark mad, let me ask you this, isn't the Messiah going to be a Jew? Even the Christians are waiting for a second coming of their savior. He came to them the first time as a Jew. Why should it be different the second time? ... Isn't the times full of signs of a new era coming?"

Marjorie had never answered that question. She had never seen Mike Eden again. But Mrs. Schwartz was a matron of Jewish benefits. She must have thought about the problem. Rachel longed to know.

But it was not the kind of thing you asked. It was not to be. The eschatological question was like sex — it was private. In the end, no one shared their private fears. But Rachel, looking at Mrs. Schwartz, realized, too, that Marjorie had never really asked this question. Despite the Jewish organizations, the benefits, the religious home, she had never really asked herself what it would mean if the Lord did come. What it would mean to her kosher food, her synagogue, her children, her grandchildren, if, in actuality, the Messiah appeared.

Rachel was stunned. How could such an obvious question, such a cataclysmic event, such a dire meaning for her and her world, escape this attractive, brighter-than-normal woman? Despite her being Jewish, it really had no importance for Marjorie Morningstar, no more importance than the far off, distantly known fact that Jesus had been crucified in the first place.

This was supposed to be one of her kind, yet, despite meeting her, Rachel was more alone than ever. *Where had the girl gone that she once was?* Where, indeed.

"Marjorie," said Rachel, "I will dedicate one of my pieces to you tonight. I will think of you as I play."

This time it was Marjorie who was touched. "How unusual," she said. "Thank you. Play it for Marjorie Morningstar, the girl who never was. Or, better, for us. No matter how different we seem. Good-bye, Rachel. It was a special pleasure meeting you. No matter what troubles you, I wish you well. Have trust in life. There are some things that are not the way they seem, no matter how keen we are on them. I'm sure you play beautifully."

Then she was gone.

Phil Green came up to her. "You're the new guitarist," he said.

"Yes," Rachel said. She remembered him as if from yesterday in *Gentlemen's Agreement*. "Things have changed."

"Not much," said Green. "A Jew still can't obtain an influential position in America."

"But look at these people," said Rachel.

"Oh, what's a few dozen senators and representatives," said Green. "Who is Kissinger or Ed Koch? A drop in the bucket. You don't see a Jew being President, do you?"

"Well," said Rachel, "Swope was head of General Electric. Irving Shapiro was president of Du Pont. Harold T. Shapiro was president of Princeton. Warren Phillips was the C.E.O. of the *Wall Street Journal*. Irving Berlin wrote "God Bless America" — I always thought it was a Jewish song, in fact."

"Exceptions," said Green. "Exceptions always prove the rule."

"What about yourself?" asked Rachel.

"O, I'm all right. If I hadn't been a Jew, I'd even be a member of the Club."

"What club?"

"Oh, you know. The Club."

"No, I don't know. I can only repeat to you what Abban Eban says: 'Jews can't take yes for an answer.'" And Rachel turned her heel on him.

"Hey," he shouted after her. "I'm a nice guy. Ask Gregory Peck."

The next day the *Times* ran a favorable review. It was signed by Adelhaide Berthold. The headline was:

DEBUT FULFILLS PRODIGY PROMISE

It said: ***Carnegie Hall Hears Sweet Notes of Sixteen.*** The article read:

Another major career was launched at Carnegie Hall last night as Rachel Rosevale, 16, of Boston, set fire to a Ramirez guitar selected personally for her in Madrid by Raul Ibiniz.

In a svelte green satin dress with a Spanish comb in her hair, the young Ms. Rosevale enchanted the auditorium. She has an unusually large sound. This is the finest guitar-playing to come along since Ibiniz, Mr. John Williams, and Mr. Julian Bream.

Playing the Bach "Suite in E-Minor" (BWW996), Ms. Rosevale was another Sharon Isbin, only more suave and less scratchy. The piece is particularly rich in keyboard texture, as it was originally written for harpsichord. Bach often transcribed cello and violin music for the lute, and the guitar is a natural for this piece. At times, Ms. Rosevale sounded almost like a harpsichord. She is a little long in the nail, but this reviewer did not find it unpleasant.

Ms. Rosevale attacked from the beginning with gusto. The prelude, with its flowing beauty of ornamental passages, immediately showed the young woman was master of her guitar. A fugue ended the movement, calling on the contrapuntal facility of both hands. Five dance movements end the piece — allemande, courante, sarabande, bourree, and gigue — and I thought Ms. Rosevale played them a little slowly, but the increased value of tone may have been worth it.

She played the lovely mystic *La Espiral Eterna* of Leo Brouwer with consummate command. The piece seemed, indeed, to spiral within itself. The work is full of cross-string sonorities and extra effects, none of which seemed to be overdone. Ms. Rosevale seemed to hold back from giving the piece temperamental value. It may be in the cool, cerebral nature of Brouwer's composition, however.

She then played a medley of dances, "*Waltz No. 3*" by Agustin Barrios, "Fandango" by Joaquin Rodrigo, "Fandanquillo" by Joaquin Turina, and "Tarantella" by Mario Castelnuovo-Tedesco.

These were competent and coloristic, but, again, the tempo was slow, though not lagging.

Ms. Rosevale's next piece was a surprisingly charming tribute of Ibiniz's composition in homage to Andres Segovia, a piece expressly written for the young prodigy and never heard in New York before. It is made up of five songs and variations, and though a little thin in comparison to more demanding pieces of the guitar repertory, it is melodic and dreamy and very suited to Ms. Rosevale's slow, loud touch.

She closed with a medley of *Bossa Nova* pieces, *Mediticao, O Passaro, Anna, Socegadamente*, and *Chega de Saudade* that were revelations when executed and phrased with this level of volume and tenderness, and, though not virtuoso pieces of great technical difficulty, were a pleasing relief from the standard showmanship of neophyte guitarists trying out their *Villa Lobos*.

In a word, Ms. Rosevale is a welcome newcomer to the major ranks and pleasing to the ear. Her teacher, Tilly Torqhardt, has done her homework and more.

19   The Confession

The next day was a free one. She had the review of the concert in her pocket, and she was somebody in this world of taxis, shops, people, hotels, and restaurants. She was at 50th Street, looking down the end of Park Avenue, and the big buildings were not intimidating, for she had a piece of paper in her pocket that was as good as an address, that had her name on it — Rachel Rosevale/ guitarist. It was as good as a card with engraved letters, and it placed her somewhere in all the skyscrapers. A person with a name, a profession, a reputation.

Besides, she had the hotel: the Waldorf Astoria. Downtown was the signature tower of Grand Central, and uptown the buildings arched away from the eye as far as one could see it was amazing to be in a city that was bigger than the eye, that stretched further than you could walk. The genteel architectural stone respectability of Park Avenue was reassuring, too — not all these windows knew you, not all these people could see you. Your life had an anonymity that left you alone, with your dignity. Yet the unknown was exciting, too.

Rachel walked slowly over to Fifth Avenue. It was still a Saturday, and the weather was a cool, sunny day, perfect for walking and window-browsing. The best shops seemed to congregate around 50th Street. She saw jumpers and suits and shoes that made elegant statements on original figures in the windows. The clothes were select and the patterns and colors a shade up on anything off the rack. She could have looked for hours. In every window she looked, she seemed to see a new Rachel stepping out smartly, without a past, with a promise of something sharp, startling, gay.

There was traffic and people around midtown, and the flags of Rockefeller Center were flying. This space amazed her. The golden statue of Prometheus and the high rise of 60 Rockefeller Center made her giddy with space and monumentality, and she promised herself lunch in the cafe and a turn on ice skates. She sauntered on past the Atlas carrying the world, the bookshop, the airlines — everywhere seemed to offer a promise of somewhere. Even St. Patrick's Cathedral, with its flying gray gothic buttresses and stone work. There seemed to be a solemnity, a dignity, a festiveness to all this, and she joined the crowd filing up and down the steps into the church.

It was very clean. The light from the stained-glass windows cast a somberness on the inside, but everything was cut and chiseled, shaped and sculpted. The wooden pews filled the aisles like stalls, and in every corner there were candles. It amused her for a moment that "Jews" rhymed with "pews." The stones were swept and washed. It was like a different world. Rachel wondered what the guitar would sound like in this sacral space.

Sacral. That was the name for it. It was a different dimension than everyday, made for light, for song, for music, for praise. She wandered down to the right transept, remembering the way the concert hall sounded the night before, and came to the Chapel of Our Lady. Our Lady was an elevated statue of a superior woman, white, sepulchral, her hand slightly raised in an eternal blessing. She could have been saying to Rachel, "Thank you for the guitar." She put to rest the usual humdrum thoughts and seemed to open a dimension of infinity, like music itself.

Beyond the chapel was the wood housing of the confessional. It looked like a house within a house and had a little orange drape over the entry. Rachel was suddenly seized by an impulse, sort of a temptation that even made her manic as it tempted her. In a half daze she approached nearer to the confessional. An old woman with rosaries came stumbling out, black scarf on her head slightly askew.

Fear gripped Rachel. For a moment she didn't know whether to go through with it. She wondered almost out loud if she were breaking a rule and what law she was insulting. Was it a Jewish law? Would Maimonides and the dead rabbis visit her with malediction? Or would the ancestors of her faith weep and wail audibly in the church if she stepped into the confessional?

Or was it a Catholic law she was breaking? Sinning against the Christians? She felt like a naughty girl who was causing some kind of unholy mixture. Was this sacrilege, unbaptized, to step into the confessional, to penetrate the curtain of sin, to speak through the screen to God's representative in the labyrinth of anonymity? Perhaps the priest would scream. Perhaps he would call the police.

She was inside. She was kneeling.

The father's voice, somewhat hoarse, came perforated through the grille.

"Yes, my daughter, what is it?"

How, Rachel suddenly wondered with fear, did he know she was a "girl? There was the sound of heavy shifting on the other side of the barrier.

Unknown to Rachel, on the other side of the grille, in his cardinalate crimson skullcap, hidden from her, was the Archbishop of New York who had the habit of still taking a few confessions incognito.

"Have you sinned?" the priest's voice came again, still perforated, as if riddled by tiny holes, through the grille.

"I am a Jew," Rachel said in a gasp.

"Ahem," the priest coughed. There was a short silence. Then he said, 'The church, when pondering her own mystery, encounters the mystery of Israel. But we believe that the promises of the Old Testament were fulfilled with the first coming of Christ."

"That's what I want," said Rachel. "I want it now."

"Ahem," said the priest. "There is baptism, my daughter. The catechism. We cannot simply have what we want. It depends on God's grace."

"I have God's grace," said Rachel. "But I don't want him to come again."

"Come again? But, of course, he'll come again. The Bible says…"

"They'll just crucify him," said Rachel in a hurry. "The Christians. It was the Roman's fault. They did it before. I want once to be for all time."

"Ahem. I cannot absolve you. You are a Jew. But I can suggest that perhaps you have not sinned."

Rachel quickly confessed. "I kissed a girl once."

"Hmmm," said the priest. "I know this is bad, but it is worse to kiss a boy."

"Tell Jesus to never come again," said Rachel urgently.

"There are bad people here. They don't want him. It will all happen again. Tell him to stay away." She was breathless.

The priest ahemmed again. "You are upset, my daughter," he said through the grille. "I cannot absolve you. But here is my card, in case you want to talk."

"I played my debut last night at Carnegie Hall," said Rachel to put things right. "It went beautifully."

"Well, that is fine. But I cannot absolve you. You should go to a rabbi," the archbishop said adjusting his crimson skullcap.

"But you are a rabbi," Rachel said.

"Ahem. A priest. Now, daughter, go in peace. Ask your God to forgive your transgression. Whatever your sin, he can rectify it. In the name of the Father, the Son, and the Holy Ghost."

She wanted to tell him more, about Harry, Grandpa Sam, and herself, to ask him who she, Rachel Rosevale, really was, and whether Christ would really recognize her. But the black grille of the confessional was dark now. She clutched the priest's card, rose from her knees, and let herself out into the great church. A father in clerical dress was standing at the other door of the confessional, looking at her, but she couldn't tell whether it was the same priest. She was confused. He seemed like a benign man, but he was in crimson, not black. The light in the church had changed. It was somehow sadder — perhaps a cloud had passed over the sun. She took the marble stones down the aisle between the near-empty pews and filed out toward the portal of the church, feeling

all the while that she had changed her destiny somehow —
had sent a message to God.

20　A Forbidden Thrill

Lenny Ratkin sipped his coffee and studied Rachel. It was unbelievable that she was still a schoolgirl — she seemed beyond it. There was something fresh about her, too, something untouched by academe that made Lenny feel in contrast like a roué. She was the first student he had ever desired, as a person that is, not just as a body. She reminded him of his Jewishness, not orthodoxy, but that inquisitiveness, that querulousness, that freedom of. mind that meant real desire for knowledge, for real knowledge. It all meant something to her, the universe, and for Lenny, the professional, it was a thrill. A forbidden thrill.

"Actually," he said, "there is a way out of your dilemma. Reform Judaism rejects the idea of a personal Messiah. He will never come. Instead, the messianic age is achieved through cooperation of all people under divine guidance. The Messiah is a collective phenomenon."

Rachel frowned. "But can a person be Jewish and not accept a personal Messiah?"

Lenny didn't want to answer. The Messiah was referred to often in both the Talmud and Midrash. Next to monotheism, it was the most important article of faith in Judaism. People neglected that, of course. He smiled bitterly. The reason was that in their heart of hearts no one knew, no one would know, how to react to the Messiah if he did come and they met him. And people know that. When the subject of the Messiah comes up, they cough, and hohum, and change the subject. Lenny did not want to say no.

"Yes," he said. But was it true? A reform Jew, sure. But a real Jew? Could a real Jew deny the personal coming of the Messiah? It was strange to Lenny because the answer was no. Yet Lenny, who didn't believe in a personal Messiah or even a collective Messiah, felt that he was a perfectly good Jew.

"It happens all the time," said Lenny lamely, wondering why this beautiful, talented girl sitting with him concerned herself about the problem at all. For a moment, it made Lenny wildly angry. Here was youth, brains, and intelligence, real sex, in fact, right in front of him, and what was happening? The child was having a problem with some doctrine in the Talmud, in the Midrash. It seemed like a waste of mental energy, no, of life, as if the old rabbinical lawyers had reached out and somehow enmeshed youth, truth, and beauty in their snares. For Lenny it was a real question, because he saw himself, if he saw anything at all, as a champion of something else, of existential enlightenment. But was he fooling himself? Was he just another rabbi interpreting the wisdom? Just another professor putting chains on the free fantasy of innocence?

"Rabbi Abiba ben Joseph," he said, "proclaimed Bar Kokhba the Messiah in the second century. He was a military leader. His insurrection failed. But he was typical of the earlier political messianism. The Jews looked for a political savior. It was only gradually that religious messianism took over from the idea of an earthly triumphant political king. That was why Jesus was rejected. He was not the expected glorious king triumphant in this world. Only slowly did the Jews come to expect a Messiah of peace, justice, and redemption. But it was too late."

"Isn't that what they want today? A political messiah?"

"No," Lenny smiled ironically. "Now they want a religious Messiah. Someone who will save them from politics. They want Jesus. A redeemer and a savior. People are sick of two thousand years of turmoil and injustice. But it is too late."

He stirred his coffee. "Do you know," he said musingly, "what the most frequently performed oratorio, the most popular extended musical composition set to English words is? It's Handel's *Messiah*, first performed in Ireland in 1742. At Christmas. Makes you think."

Rachel looked at him. "Why should that be?" she asked.

"'He shall feed his flock and I know that my Redeemer liveth,'" Lenny quoted.

He looked tired. But Rachel thought the lines around his face were attractive. They were like scars of battle. He appeared to her like a champion of intelligence, and it was handsome.

"Lenny, I'm scared," she said.

"Of what?"

"That he will come."

Lenny laughed.

"Don't you see?" she said.

"You mean nobody will recognize him?"

"No. They will. That's the trouble. They'll crucify him."

"Crucifixion is dead."

"No. They'll resurrect it. They'll do it again."

Lenny still laughed.

Rachel blushed. "You should know it yourself, Lenny. You're the master of irony, of skepticism, of doubt, of cynicism."

"I...," Lenny saw that she was serious.

"Would you have done it to Jesus?" she asked.

He leaned forward. "We killed him, Rachel. And you know why? Because he didn't want to be a doctor."

Rachel smiled wanly. But it was a tired joke. She had heard it before. Yet it was funny. She couldn't help it. "Or a lawyer," she said. But something went out of her. She lost a little of her faith in Lenny.

21 The Locked Door

Lenny took her to his top floor duplex apartment in a new office building that was empty at night. Downstairs it said "Professor Ratkin" in white plastic lettering in the directory. There was not a soul about.

The elevator slid smoothly up to the top floor, where a foyer with a small oriental rug and a potted plant dressed the entrance to the apartment. It was all very respectable, but quiet. He let her in with a slight brush of his hand on her shoulder. She trudged in, carrying her black guitar case.

Inside, he switched on the lights. They were overhead spots, like a gallery, and the walls were white. The furnishings were spare but comfortable modern, and the decor was aesthetic. The pictures on the walls were set off distinctively, given value, and obviously Lenny was a collector of sorts. Rachel looked at several and murmured something.

"Well," said Lenny, "they're not the expressionists, but I do what I can on Newbury Street. They're like pets. Or poems. Each picture is some kind of memory."

"You were never married?" Rachel asked.

"No," said Lenny abruptly. "I mean, there was a girl once. But *c'est la vie*. She ran off with a Frenchman. Left me badly burned."

Rachel looked at more paintings. They were truly well-chosen, a mix of texture, abstraction, and some surrealism. She looked at a picture of a naked young blond man, godlike, with his back to a woman in blue who was reading to him from a book.

"Magic realism," said Lenny. "It's illusion made realer than reality."

It seemed to describe his apartment. She wondered if music could be magic realism. While he went into the kitchenette to fix coffee and a drink, she got her new guitar, the Ramirez that Harry had bought her for her sixteenth birthday. It was spring. A slight, soft breeze came in from the window. She began to warm up.

Lenny came back in, went to the window, and shut it, then went to the door. He sat down across from her. "Coffee will be ready in a minute. Play."

First she played *Lagrima* — the tear-drop. It was in the key of E, a short piece. A melancholic, romantic song. She didn't know why she played it, but it seemed to fit the hush. It was a two-part Andante piece, and she played it with lingering sorrow, as if it would break her heart. Lenny was astounded. Her guitar seemed to fill the room.

"Francisco Tarrega," she said when she finished.

"Continue."

She launched into a longer, much harder, modern piece by Leo Brouwer, *La Espiral Eterna* — the Eternal Spiral. Brouwer was born in Havana in 1939. He was a colorist but also an admirer of Bach. The piece imitated the improvisatory freedom of the Baroque. It had a dazzling array of cross-string sonorities with a dance-like rhythm fused together by a Southern night. The piece sounded like a mysterious spiral unraveling, with oscillating strings and a pizzicato, fingerboard tapping, and muffled notes. It created an illusion of eternity.

Lenny was watching her sharply. He had never heard anything like it. It seemed to come off her fingernails like some marvelous improvisation on the nervous system. He was alert. The notes wreaked of love, virginal love. It was like something from the temples of antiquity, and Lenny was reminded of the virgin priestesses.

She stopped.

Lenny's eyes made her uncomfortable. They were penetrating. She felt suddenly exposed, although, somehow, she had played especially well, as if his eyes gave her an added edge.

"I'll get the coffee," he said finally. "Brava."

They sat huddled by the coffee table, and Rachel told him the story of her new guitar. Tilly Torqhardt had sent Raul Ibeniz, the famous Spanish concertist, personally to the Ramirez shop in Madrid to select an instrument for her. She had the guitar insured for five thousand dollars and shipped over to Rachel for her birthday. Harry had made the presentation, reading Lorca's poem.

The Guitar

The weeping
of the guitar begins.
Wineglasses shatter
in the dead of night...
It's useless
to hush it...
It's impossible
to hush it.
It weeps for things

far, far away.
For the sand of the hot South
that begs for white camellias...
Oh, guitar!
Heart gravely wounded
by five swords.

Rachel didn't know why, but all her sixteenth birthday images had had to do with tears, not that she had been sad. Was it some kind of prophecy? She had shuddered at the poem and shuddered again as she told it to Lenny.

Suddenly Lenny picked up his wineglass from the table and drank off, then he put the glass on the floor. "We shall see," he said. And, while she watched, he picked up his foot and smashed the glass. The crunch of tinkling glass punctuated the music that had been.

The symbolism shocked Rachel. It had been in the poem — *"Wineglasses shatter/ in the dead of night."*

"What was that for?" Rachel asked.

"A Jewish wedding," said Lenny, an ironic, hard smile playing on his attractive lips.

"A Jewish wedding?" Rachel said, her eyes growing large.

Lenny leaned forward and ran her soft, auburn hair through his fingers. "You've never slept with a man, have you?"

Rachel, scared, looked back at him.

"The music was incredible," Lenny said. "You're just incredible. It's like magic realism."

He kissed her on the couch. It was a hard, ironic, mature kiss. It took her breath away. "I shouldn't have come here," she said.

"Maybe not," said Lenny.

He kissed her again. It aroused her, but this time she struggled. He bent her arms back and took his time. She wrestled free.

Lenny laughed. "You can leave anytime you want," he said, kissing her again.

"I'd better," she said, standing up. Her hair was messed and her dress was skewed.

"Play another song," Lenny urged her, playfully. But she packed her guitar.

"Good night, Lenny," she said, trotting to the door.

He smiled.

The door was locked from the inside. She shook the knob. It turned, but the door wouldn't open. Lenny was coming toward her. She turned pale. There was no smile on his face.

"It's a French trick," he said.

"I'll scream," Rachel answered.

Lenny smiled again. "Scream all you want. Nobody will hear you. The building is empty at night."

He took her wrists, hard. She tried to shout, but it was as if a clamp had tightened around her throat. Nothing would come out. She made a pathetic little whistling noise, like a bird. She looked at him. He was not ugly. He was calm. He was still Professor Lenny Ratkin and she felt a terrible weakness overcoming her.

"It's easy," he said, still wrenching her wrist. "There's one way not to get hurt. It's your choice."

She looked at him, terrified. But he meant it. His face was absolutely serious, a terrible hunger on it, and he looked at her exactly as if she were a bird of prey.

"There's nothing to it," he said. "Take your clothes off." And he took the guitar from her. He handled it with tender care, laying it on the table beside the door. "Well?" he said. "Do I have to hurt you?"

Rachel, trancelike, came back into the room. He took a menacing step toward her and raised his arm. It seemed like some kind of a dream, but she didn't want him to hit her. She unbuttoned the top of her dress, not thinking it was real. *Illusion that is realer than reality.* Her motions were mechanical as she looked unbelievingly at him. The trouble was Lenny was not transformed. He was still Professor Lenny Ratkin. He took off his tweed jacket and threw it on the chair. Then he turned to her. "Do it. Or do you want help?"

After that she didn't really remember. He came towards her and helped her take the dress off. She was sixteen. Rachel was a full girl. Her birthday had been portentous with tears. She was standing there in her underclothes, socks, and shoes.

"Take off your shoes," he said.

She did as she was told. Again he grabbed her wrist, but this time firmly, soberly. She was not even conscious of what he did. She scarcely seemed to be there any longer. It was as if it were unreal. Far away. Did not belong to her.

He reached down and slid her panties down her legs. She thought she would fall. His hand slipped firmly between her legs and he spread her.

"Undo your brassier," he told her.

Blindly, she obeyed. Her full breasts fell out and the garment fell to the floor. He brushed a hand over her nipple and involuntarily it hardened. She had no more strength. No more command. Again he took her wrist strongly and bent her toward the couch. She sank to her knees. Without knowing it, she was crying. But he pulled her up and fondled her breasts and took her under the armpits. He jammed a knee in her crotch and pushed her back on the couch.

"It's all right, Rachel," he said. "Beautiful Rachel. *The weeping of the guitar begins.* You were wise not to resist."

She was wet between the legs. He reached down with his hand and spread her knees. She had her eyes closed.

Somehow, if she closed her eyes, nothing would open. If she kept her eyes closed, she wasn't there. He took her panties the rest of the way off and spread her legs. She was whimpering. It wasn't Lenny anymore. It was just a man. A brute. An apartment. She had almost lost consciousness, but another part of her was counting the seconds. It would not be forever. She would get out of here. He took her hand and laid it on his manhood. She had never felt anything so stiff and large and hard. Then he wasn't there anymore. She wasn't there anymore. She wasn't even Rachel. And he had her.

22   The Loft

Afterwards, Rachel went to Rick's. She was not numb, but strung-out. It had made her alert. The knowledge that she was no longer a virgin was like someone else's biography. Something fatalistic about Rachel kept her from being personally mad at Lenny — it was just the way he was. It didn't even surprise her. If anything, he had been sort of smart. She had been dumb. She was surprised that Lenny had a streak of cruelty, but she admitted that he used it cleverly. Rachel did not have ideas that the world was particularly kind, that nice things happen, that people are gently. She took it as it came. The world was what it turned out to be. That was Lenny. Dumb, yes, she saw herself that way. Innocent, gullible, taken-advantage-of, hurt, too, but not wounded, not dead, still walking — if it was violation, still she was matter-of-fact about it.

When she got to the loft, Rick opened the door. It was eerie. The silence was the same. The building was empty.

"What happened to you?" Rick said.

"Nothing," she answered.

He looked so considerate. So unhurried. So cool. She even recognized that she desired him, although what it was she was looking for was not so clear to her. Shelter? Perhaps to get away from Lenny, from the scene at the duplex, from her stupidity, from her shame. She wanted to put things right, to put the margins — the parameters, they would say, or was it perimeter? — back on life, back from the door that had threatened to open at Lenny's into real brutality. In the end, he had not been actually brutal himself, but he offered a choice: brutality or himself. She had chosen Lenny.

But now she wanted Rick. To make it good. To soften the awful choice she had been through. Lenny, the professor; Rick, the student. She had had a reality lesson. Now she wanted to make it up to Rick, without his ever knowing. To assure Rick that reality was not the way it was. To marginalize the professor's world. To forget. To reassure herself.

"Well, hey. A little messed up, aren't we?"

She kissed him.

"What good thing has gotten into you?" he murmured.

She kissed him again, to keep him quiet. "Don't talk," she said. "Just be with me."

Then she saw the bass. "I know what," she said. "Let's play *Socegadamente*." Bossa nova. The title meant, "softly."

"Now?" said Rick.

"Please."

They got out their instruments. Actually, Rachel, when she had left Lenny's had almost forgotten her guitar — "My guitar, please," she had said at the last moment, by the door. "By all means," Lenny had said, handing her the black case. At least she had salvaged something. "Come again," he had said, smiling.

Socegadamente was a soft piece, easy, lilting, high on the first string. Rick alternated between bass and drums. Rachel took comfort in her fingers. It was as if the elasticity and agility overcame her shock. A great cure for rape. Because that's what it had been, practically. If she hadn't done it, perhaps that's what it would have been. Or had he bluffed it? What if she hadn't gotten scared, if she had just said no, would he have just burst out laughing? Nice try, man. Or had she secretly wanted to? That was another catch, the unconscious. *Something* had attracted her, *something* had drawn her to him all those months, and that lecturing, all those coffees, and now she knew. She had found out. It takes flying into the flame to singe your wings.

They played *Socegadament* at least ten times.

"When!" Rick said finally. "What brought that on?"

"I needed that. Rick, make love to me." Rachel stood up.

"I thought you didn't want to," he said.

"I changed my mind," she said, and she took off her blouse.

"Don't ask," she said. "Just do it, Rick." And she took him by the hand and led him behind the partition to the loft's bed.

"I want you to have me," Rachel said, taking the rest of her clothes off. "Tonight. Just hold me. I'm yours."

Rick knew there was something wrong with it, but he knew, too, that he dare not ask. He had been dreaming of this since he sat beside Rachel at Professor Ratkin's first class, but he didn't know what to say. He wanted to quote from Spinoza, because God seemed to be a part of this; at least Rick hoped God was part of it, because Rick had made a shrewd bet with himself: that sex was spiritual, not a sin, like the Church said. And if it was spiritual, it had to do with love, and love had to do with the spirit — but the sight of Rachel's body, beautiful in the half-shadow coming through door and lighting the bed, confirmed to him what he was looking for, which wasn't a duality, a polarity of good and evil, but an integration: a simultaneousness of the body and the mind. He put his hand on her knee. He wanted to say all this to her and more, but he couldn't think of any words.

Then he muttered, "You're the first Jewish girl I've ever had."

It was a terribly silly thing to say. He didn't even know why Christianity entered his mind at this moment. It wasn't what he meant to say. It was absurd.

Rachel only lay back. "Don't talk, Rick. Just have me. I'm yours."

She knew what a lie it was. She knew, in fact, that it was just the kind of irony that Professor Lenny Ratkin would appreciate. But she couldn't help it. And she knew that if she said anything more, anything else, she would be lost. He was very tentative at first. She folded him in her arms. The strange thing was that now she was the woman, and he was the boy. The difference was that he actually loved her. *Socegadamente*. Perhaps they should have played *Desafinado* — "slightly out of tune." But slowly he got the hang of it until, pent up, strung out, she had an orgasm that released him, and herself, and again, but she remained dry-eyed, even when he went to sleep, and she remained awake, holding this big, tender boy, thinking that she had had Lenny's orgasm, the orgasm that Lenny had produced, the shock, the shame, the thrill, delayed, not with the professor, but with Rick. And she felt better.

Only something was still wrong. She realized in the dark that she was hungry. Her mouth watered. She could have used a good delicatessen.

23   In the Cafeteria

The next time Rachel saw Lenny, he was in the Brandeis cafeteria, and anger welled in her heart as he came over to her table and set his tray down. He didn't say a thing, as if there were no need to. As if it had never happened. Rachel spoke first.

"God was an adulterer," she said. She was almost tempted to say "rapist." Somehow this gave her satisfaction, though she knew it was theological casuistry. She had tried the same argument out on Rick, but it didn't wash. He said she was not being spiritual.

"How so?" said Lenny, an ironic grin creasing one corner of his mouth.

"The Lord made love to Mary, Joseph's wife."

"Oh, ho ho," said Lenny. "The penis did not enter the vagina, so, technically, it was not sexual intercourse. No sexual intercourse, ergo no adultery."

"There's where you're wrong, Lenny," said Rachel. "Because Jesus Christ himself says, 'But I say onto you, that whoever looketh on a woman to lust after her hath committed adultery with her already in his heart.' So God committed adultery in his heart."

"You have to understand purity, Rachel," Lenny said. "God looked on her purely."

Rachel couldn't believe her ears, that this was coming from Lenny.

"Why did God," she said, "after making a covenant with Abraham and Isaac against human sacrifice, accept Jesus Christ's sacrifice?"

Lenny didn't think long. "Because God is a Christian," he said, half tongue in cheek.

God, a Christian? She had always thought of God as Jewish. But Lenny had a point — a Jewish God would not sacrifice a man.

Lenny looked pleased that he had stumped her. "Only a Christian would sacrifice a God," he said.

"A man," Rachel retorted.

"The Jewish God does not condone human sacrifice."

"It was self-sacrifice," Rachel suggested.

"Suicide?" said Lenny. "Hmmm. The Jewish God does not condone suicide, either."

Rachel was silent. It seemed that they were doomed to argue about God, not themselves — that the subject of themselves was too delicate to broach. Instead, the argument about God took on something vicious between them.

"Look," said Lenny. "The whole thing was the fault of the Roman Empire. Pontius Pilate was a bureaucrat."

Lenny was trying to be funny. Rachel was still silent. He continued, "Christians and Jews, to be ecumenical, like to say they have the same God. But Jewish Gods don't sacrifice men. Beside, Yahweh has no son. So the whole rigmarole that the God of Abraham and the God of the gentiles is the same is untrue."

"You mean, I have to choose Gods?" Rachel asked.

"Save yourself the trouble. Stay Jewish."

What Rachel wanted, she realized now, was a Jewish God, but with a son — Jesus Christ. Otherwise, as a Jew, she would have to accept that Yahweh had sacrificed a Jewish man, Jesus, a marginal Jew, unjustly, and for no reason at all. She didn't want an unreasonable God.

"Forget it, Rachel. He was just a rabble-rouser. He made trouble for the temple."

"So," she said, "what about you?"

Lenny laughed bitterly.

They were both silent a moment. The night that had been between them was present like a shadow they could not talk about. A dead God seemed to be the only thing they could talk about. All Rachel's vehemence went into the argument, as if religion were a surrogate for talking about themselves.

"Look what the past led to!" Rachel suddenly cried. "Arguments. Who could eat with whom? Look what the confusion about Jesus led to: Christian arrogance, persecution of the Jews. Yet this is nothing compared to what could happen when he comes again. His coming might go unheralded, a tragedy, or he could be re-crucified. The Jews could welcome him and start to persecute Christians or Arabs. He might not be recognized as the same old Messiah by some. He might be recognized as a new Messiah by others. Some might call Christ anti-Christ. Others might recognize the anti-Christ, if he comes, as Christ. It's a nightmare.

Now Lenny was silent.

"So why not embrace Jesus?" Rachel went on. "He was a Jew. You're a Jew if you believe in Jesus. Ha. Ha. Religions have been based on less. After all, there's nothing else that unifies Jews anymore. Throw out God, throw out the laws, throw out the temple — some Jews have already done that. A Jewish mother? Why not Jesus? He had a Jewish mother. Jesus tried to emancipate Jews once from the rigidities of law, from the temple, from fanaticism. Why do postmodernist Jews have to go through the same story again? Belief in Jesus would be simpler. Jesus as a Son of Man. That would unify and emancipate Jews. It would do something for Christians, too. It would solve the problem of Jewish identity. It would solve the prophecies and fulfill the myth of the Jewish archetype of suffering, exile, atonement, disaster, and salvation. Jesus — God of the holocaust."

Lenny was still silent.

Rachel leaned forward. "They stole our religion, Lenny. The Christians stole our God. A Jew. Why not? Should we walk around in shadows and guilt all our lives just because some Jews don't like Jesus? Just because Lenny says no? He was the classic Jew! He's their own. Even the Arabs might buy him."

"You're shouting," said Lenny.

"I am not shouting!" Rachel shouted back. "I'm dead serious. The Jews have an identity problem. Make the Israeli litmus test for being a Jew belief in a Jew, in Jesus. It's better than having the Jewish lawyers in Israel rejecting the sons of Jewish fathers. Would Jesus have rejected them? If God was Jesus' father, and Mary was Joseph's wife, then, according to Jewish law, Jesus is a *mamser*, a bastard, anyway.

Don't let the lawyers and rabbis decide the fate of your child! Believe in the Jew: Jesus. He showed all Jews how to live and die. He went to the right hand of the Lord to sit. I'm tired of having Christians enjoy the fruits of Christianity without paying homage to Jews. No wonder they killed Jews. They didn't even know their own God was a Jew. And the Jews don't know it themselves. How dumb can you be?"

"Come on, Rachel. Laugh a little," Lenny said.

"No. You say that all revelation is edited by human beings. Not even the Bible was transmunicated directly by God. Historicity. In other words, Torah, the Old Testament, is qualified human words."

"Yes."

"All right. Jesus' words were human."

She didn't go on. She expected him to react. But he didn't get the point.

"God, you're dumb," she said. "I thought you were the mouth of truth itself. God's word. You haven't even thought about it!"

"I don't see what you're driving at."

"Jesus, Lenny. Jesus was human. You're so busy denying Jesus' divinity, you don't even see that he actually lived. Historicity, Lenny. You're against Jesus because he was God. I'm for him because he was human."

"But…"

"Development, Lenny. Historical development. Jesus was a historical development of Judaism. You're always so adamant about Torah not being the literal word of God. You say reality was edited by human beings. Well, that's what Jesus did. He edited reality. He spoke man's words, Lenny. The Passion. You're so busy denying God that you don't hear man!"

"But," Lenny finally said, "the rabbis argue that the law is *infallible* because it comes from God. The Catholics pronounce God's *infallible* word. But it's all history. It began. It developed. The situation changed. It's not God's word. That's the point of historical criticism."

"Lame, Lenny," said Rachel. "The man actually lived and died. Men told the story. It's called the Passion, and just because you can make God go away with all your hocus pocus about historical criticism, you can't make man go away. You can't sweep Jesus under the rug. Man, if not God, is infallible. Even if he was nobody."

"Jesus never claimed that," said Lenny limply.

"That's the point, Lenny. He was human."

She eyed him wearily as only a woman can eye a man that she has had.

"Righteousness and uprightness. That's Jewish," said Rachel to Lenny. "You probably think it's some kind of erection, but you're wrong. It's a feeling. A kind of health. And women can have it, too."

24 Characterological Disorder

Rachel wasn't eating again. A long shroud of thought covered her days, and Deborah could not stand it. She called Dr. Themagorsky. He had helped her once. He was a big, burly man with a trimmed gray beard and spectacles. He looked the part of a psychiatrist, as if he might have personally known Freud.

This time their meeting was difficult. Rachel went to his office at Private Hospital and pictured herself among the patients on the lawns. The wards were locked off. It said, as she passed the second floor ward on the way up to Themagorsky's, "Beware of door; split risk." There was an eerie silence about the place and gloom lay laden in the corridors and halls like a kind of soup.

She had to wait in the hall for the doctor and idly skipped through the magazines. Every fresh face, staff or patient, raised the question, "Is this person a crazy or not?" Rachel wondered if she looked instantaneously recognizable, like a patient. There was something blotchy, unfocussed about their faces, as if they belonged there, misfits, while the staff people bustled purposively up and down the halls. Which was Rachel? On which side?

The doctor came out and fetched her. A consultation. That was what they were having. He settled her in a chair and then returned to behind his desk. Rachel noticed the photos of his wife and children, and this seemed to define normalcy — a wife and children. But Rachel had no wife and children. How should she begin? "I am not crazy, doctor. But I want to be hospitalized anyway, because the world isn't safe."

No. Dr. Themagorsky stared at her silently, waiting.

"I know I am not the Messiah," Rachel suddenly blurted out.

"Hummph," said Dr. Themagorsky. "How do you know that?"

Rachel had not expected this response. "Because they'll crucify the Messiah," she said.

Dr. Themagorsky played with a pencil. "Tell me, Rachel, do you hear voices?"

Rachel was prepared for this one. Judy Kaplan had told her they always asked that: "Do you hear voices?" and "Do you want to kill yourself?" as if it helped to ask.

"I hear your voice," Rachel said.

"Hurnmph. I mean, voices in the air telling you to do things?"

"No." Rachel lied. Of course, she heard voices. A voice told her what time it was. A voice told her to go to the bathroom. A voice corrected her guitar. A voice told her they would crucify the Messiah when he came. "No," she repeated. "I don't hear voices. I hear your voice."

"So when did this begin?" asked the doctor. "When did you begin thinking about the Messiah?"

"You don't understand. I am not the Messiah. I don't think I am the Messiah," said Rachel.

"Then what's the problem?"

"I want to be let into the hospital."

"Hummph. If you're not the Messiah, why should we let you into the hospital? We don't let just anybody in." This little pleasantry fell flat.

There was a pause. Finally Dr. Themagorsky broke it. "I know you are not the Messiah, if that is any help. A sense of reality is a support. But neither must you underrate yourself."

"But," said Rachel, "if it suited their purposes, they would make me into one."

"Into what?"

"The Messiah."

"The Messiah?"

"Yes. By political appointment. Now that Israel is a state, they have the power. Perhaps there is a purpose. Suddenly the Messiah is in their interest, not God's."

"But you are a girl."

"Ha! Ha!" Rachel laughed. "They could pick anyone. The weaker the better. The Shekinah is female. She is a kind of Holy Ghost that broods over Jerusalem."

Dr. Themagorsky coughed. "But Isaiah has said, 'The believer shall not make haste.'"

"They are not believers," Rachel said bitterly. "They will do whatever suits them."

Rachel was young, but she knew she was being overly serious. Only when a religion can laugh at itself can it be redeemed from fanaticism. She knew this to be true, yet it could not save her from herself. A joke was too holy for her to consider that she herself was the joke.

"Probably he was the Christ the first time," said Rachel. "Otherwise, why would they have done it? Doesn't the book say prophecies have to be fulfilled?"

Dr. Themagorsky looked sour. He swiveled in his chair. "Rachel, I'll be frank with you. You don't have a personality disorder. You have a characterological disorder. You do not have delusions of grandeur. You have *fear* of illusions of grandeur. Do I make myself clear?"

Rachel gulped.

"Now I can't admit you to the hospital. If you thought you were the Messiah, we could let you in, but all I can do is give you a tranquilizer, if you want one. Maybe you have been working too hard, but I don't want to keep you from your guitar. Many people have characterological disorders. We can live with these things if we try. I suggest I see you again in, say, two weeks? How is that?"

A characterological disorder. Was being a Jew a characterological disorder? Folk paranoia. But she wasn't paranoid. Neither was Harry. This was reality she was talking about.

And why two weeks? Was the situation going to get any better in two weeks? Was Israel going to change? Was the Messiah going to decide in two weeks not to come? The truth was the world didn't make any sense. That was the trouble. And the doctor called it a characterological disorder.

Part Three

25   A Dybbuk

If Harry could have had a swan song, what would it have been: civil rights, civil liberties, abortion, foreign aid, social welfare, separation of Church and State, the politics of life and death, world justice, democracy, or social justice? Or was the Jewish liberal extinct?

Liberalism, paradoxically, for a Jew, argued against intolerance towards other groups; in fact, it argued for others as individuals rather than as groups, argued that *religious* and *ethnic* differences were an anachronism.

Was the Jew simply to die out, thin out into the pluralist populace until he was submerged, vanished, the chosen people disseminated across the earth like dust? The ever-dying people? They would all be *pentalayids* eventually, the whole human race, the Hebrew word for those who have a drop in the blood — like the dot on the i in Israel.

Or was Harry, secretly, sentimentally, a frustrated Hasid, a pious one longing for Sam's memories, for the ghetto, for the black coat and hat, the ringlets, the book, the songs? Sometimes drilling teeth, he thought of these things. He remembered one patient who, after having a mouthful of rotten teeth removed and replaced, begrudgingly called him "a benefactor of mankind." He would like to think so. It was more useful than trading diamonds in New York or Tel Aviv.

Maybe what he really wanted, though, was the mysticism, joy, and sense of community of the Hasidim, without their sexism, fundamentalism, and authoritarianism.

Or should he have been a new Jew, an Israeli, reclaiming the Promised Land, turning today into tomorrow, building the New Jerusalem?

Or should he have been an American, a believer in the red, white, and blue, the stars, and the pursuit of life, liberty, and happiness? What did it mean, in the new Millennium, to be an American? Were T.V., bubble gum, cars, money, and violence really enough? Was all of that a way of life? What had happened to the source of American values — what were those values anyway? Freedom of worship? Harry was pious, but he didn't worship. What sources did those American values have? Capitalism, competition, materialism? No. Those came later. The military and the world wars?

Harry had recently seen the President visit Boston. It was alarming. The newspaper carried a picture on the front page of him kissing a baby, but that wasn't the real story. The real story was the security. <u>That</u> was the picture. Five hundred motorcycle cops in full regalia, bulletproof limousines, the black killer wagon sprouting automatics in all directions, the pistol-packing police, the F.B.I, in gray plainclothes, their underarm holsters padding their suits, the mounted cavalry, boots on, guns ready, holding the crowd back, penned behind barricades, the Secret Service men everywhere and atop the buildings with six-foot binoculars scanning the crowd. The

President didn't even roll down the tinted glass that hid him from view. The motorcade drove too fast. It was ominous. This was America? This was the people? This was democracy? Or had Sam made a mistake? Why did not one of the newspapers or agencies see that this — after all, they saw it easily enough in Germany or Russia — was the real story, the picture opportunity, the shocker?

America, the free — or Amerika, the land of the paramilitary?

"The United States is our Palestine," said Rabbi David Philipsen, arrested in 1995, "and Washington our Jerusalem." Was he, after all, wrong?

Harry remembered with chagrin reading Grandpa Sam the "I am an American" statement when he reached twenty-one. And now?

What about Rachel? The girl was planning her Israeli trip to Jerusalem. She had been invited by the Rubin Academy to play a concerto, the *Concerto of the Oranges*, with the Jerusalem Symphony Orchestra in the Henry Crown Hall. She had been reading all kinds of literature and asking him all kinds of questions. But, alas, always on her mind was the question of the Messiah.

She looked up Herschel — what is a Jew? Not Feldman's American secular spirit, but the spirit of protest of great prophets against a confusion of the true God with many early idols. That only made things worse for her. "To be a Jew," Herschel said, "is to renounce allegiance to false gods; to be sensitive to God's infinite stake in every finite situation; to bear witness to this presence in the hours of His concealment; to remember the world is unredeemed. We are born to be an answer to this question." That was why Rachel was born tomorrow.

But then she showed him the poster from the Committee for the Messiah, based in Israel. It showed a man in a black coat with a long beard and black hat, and an air force pilot in goggles and gear, pointing — like Uncle Sam in the old war posters — "I want <u>you</u>."

"I have a *dybbuk* within me speaking," she told Harry. "It asks me all the time if I want to be the Messiah and die on the cross."

Harry told her not to listen to the evil spirit, that she didn't have to ask what the purpose of her trip was. Life had given her a purpose. She had a calendar. She was the function of what she did. Her identity was not dependent on some other factor. On being a Jew. On making *Aliyah* to Israel. It was not a question of what Israel is, or America. It did not matter if she was orthodox or socialist or liberal. She was a guitar player.

"Is that the same as being a wandering Jew?" she asked.

No, he said, the guitar gave her a specific identity. It relieved her of the burden of ethnic identity, of racial guilt, of religious anguish. One did not need Abraham and David as much if one had one's guitar.

But Harry could not convince himself. He was scared for the Messiah, too. It was too much for a person. He also sensed the emptiness of the special pleading, ethnocentrism, and shoddy thinking that marked the great upsurge in ethnic studies programs. The studies' purpose was the search for objectivity, not ethnic and religious consciousness-raising. But this was often self-defeating. The bread of Europe is different from Wonder Bread because the salt, the water, the air, the humidity, the flour, are different — old Jewish rye may taste better, be more real. The same with Jewishness. The songs, the customs, the ghetto, the Sabbaths were different — they used to be "real." In America, they became replicas. The bread didn't taste as good. Bingo, and auctions. The religion wasn't real. It wasn't the Wailing Wall. The candle didn't shimmer the same as in olden times. Instead, there were studies. Sociological truth substituted for living reality. The life was gone. America was a cold and heady ersatz for the *hora*, for the real dance.

That was one Harry, the son of Grandpa Sam. The other Harry was, surprisingly, an optimist in Jewish matters. He believed Jews could survive without ghetto walls. He saw a vibrant Jewish life in freedom in the United States, the country of rationalist and universalistic values of the Enlightenment.

He didn't even think Jews needed a personal Messiah. Redemption could be the collective consciousness of Jews, even of the whole world, bringing about a better world. "Maybe it has already begun," he told Rachel.

"What about the ancient Jewish prayer?" she reminded him. "I believe with all my heart in the coming of the Messiah and even if he be delayed, nevertheless I shall wait for him every day."

Harry felt a certain impatience. Besides, he didn't feel well.

"Sam used to say a Jew learns what not to do but not what to do," Harry told her, as if that would help.

"To be a Jew in America," she read to him from Leonard Fein,, "is to carry with you the consciousness of limitless savagery. It is to carry that consciousness with you not as an abstraction, but as a reality; not, God help us all, only as a memory, but also as possibility."

"In America?" Harry's head swam. He really wasn't feeling well. He wanted a milkshake. It was this kind of thing that led Harry to stop giving to Jewish funds for a year at a time.

It was people like Fein who create the wrong possibility. Reverse racism, in Harry's mind, was a sickness of the soul.

Yet Harry refused to weaken the memory, too. The memory is redemption, according to an old Jewish saying. Harry wanted to keep the memory but not prejudice the possibilities.

Life. Not death. That was the Jewish choice. The atrocities could not be forgotten, but if pain, suffering, and victimization became the only images for the future, the enemy would win. Honor was not possible if the Jews remembered too little; life was not possible if they remembered too much. This was why one dance of the hora moved Harry more than all the reminders of the holocaust. Harry didn't want history to rob him of joy.

This, too, was why the Hasidim, with their sacred purpose, made more of an impression on Harry than the nineteen museums, forty-eight resource centers, twelve memorials, twenty-six research institutes, and five libraries in the United States dedicated to the holocaust. A tissue of tears. To Harry it was more important to wipe away the tears than drown in them. The Hasidim lived for something, an energy, a Jewish energy, while the holocaust industry festered in horror.

Rachel read him another snippet. "This is from 'Israel without Apology,'" she said. "Michael J. Rosenberg. He says, 'In dealing with those who oppose Israel, we are not reasonable and we are not rational. Nor should we be.'"

It was too much. His head swam. He had no argument. He only wanted a milkshake. Then Rachel told him redemption began with the building of the third temple. But after 1967, militant radical rabbis proclaimed that the Messianic days were near. Then, in 1985, Jewish underground fundamentalists were caught trying to blow up the Arab Dome of the Rock to make way for the third temple. A Passover sacrifice of a paschal lamb on the altar of the temple mount is said to hasten the coining of the Messiah.

Harry wondered why it couldn't stop. He held his head between his hands.

Then she read him Rabbi Meir Kahane's statement from *Ha'aretz*, the Israeli newspaper. "We have it in our power to bring the Messiah," the rabbi said.

Harry's head was splitting. "Goddamn Israel," he muttered.

Suddenly he collapsed. Rachel could not catch him. He hit the floor, but now he was gurgling, "O hear, O Israel…"

It was in Room 301 of Brigham and Women's Hospital that Rachel learned her own secret.

Harry was on his deathbed. He had gone very quickly. Rachel could see him slipping away by the minute.

"I have something to tell," Harry said, barely audible.

Rachel came nearer. "I'm not your father," said Harry.

There was a long pause.

"It was Rabbi Solovetch." Harry swallowed. "At least that's what Deborah thinks."

Rachel looked at him. The shock had not hit her yet, but slowly she saw herself fading away. She was losing something she wasn't even sure she loved, but she was sure now.

"You know why I tell you?" Harry whispered.

"Why?" said Rachel.

"Because a momser can't be the Messiah." Harry ludicrously grinned. "So being a bastard saves you. But the rabbi doesn't know. So it's up to you. The law is on your own conscience. Nobody knows but you and I."

Rachel thought of the irony of it being her own conscience, and an absurd image of a trial arose in her where she was accused of being the Messiah, but then the judge asked her, "Are you a momser?" A bastard? What would she answer? If she had the opportunity to save the world, would it be enough to answer, "No. I can't do it. You see, I'm a bastard."

Harry gurgled. He looked serious again. "The funny thing is that it didn't save Jesus. At least that's what I've always believed. He was the son of Ben Pandera, the Roman soldier. I'm sure of it. Jesus was a bastard."

"That's an old wives' tale," said Rachel. "It comes from the Jewish middle ages, the *Ishot Jeshua*."

"Still, it's a good story," said Harry. "Ha. Ha. But being a bastard will save <u>you</u>. The rabbis, in a sense, rejected Jesus, too. And you, a momser; they'll reject you, too. So don't worry about it, even if you're not my mopsy."

Rachel began to cry.

Harry made an effort. "I'm sorry, Rachel. The girl that stole her father's images. I tell you, Rachel, marry Lenny. He may be Jewish, which is good, but he's fallen far enough so that no rabbi will object if a momser marries him. Lenny is man enough for a civil ceremony. And at least he's circumcised, even if it's not his own fault. Your children will never be able to enter the assembly of the Eternal One anyway, because of Rabbi Solovetch, so don't worry. Maybe Jesus will save you, after all. He could even save Lenny." Another smile curled on Harry's lip.

"You can't save the world, girl," Harry's eyes begged her, "but you can save Lenny."

There was more sadness in the moment, more courage and life than Rachel's nice little religion was prepared for. Saying nice little things sounded empty. She had to look into her heart of spiritual values and realize she was passing a dud watch off on Harry, a toy. Life was greater, grander, and more awesome than she had let herself believe. There was more love but also more indifference than she suspected. So, sitting with Harry, her sentimental religion was dying like his body. It was only when she admitted she had nothing sustaining to say that a flash of recognition leapt between the bed and her. She and Harry looked at each other and knew they were in the same boat. Against her will she was forced to grow up. Rachel had to grow into adulthood while Harry had to grow into eternity. This was what it meant to be there and to be dying — to serve. Death cut the die on life. It framed what had been. The truth was not cozy, but it made you free. It even made her pray deeper, not to Harry, but for the shelter of God's presence, for Harry and for herself.

She looked at him a long time. His affliction only impressed on her own inadequacy. Death seemed surrounded by a conspiracy of silence. For some problems there just is no answer. It's no use trying to invent one. Religion hadn't taught her that. Reality had. It was clear when she tried to be cheerful for Harry that she was trying to cheer herself. The amazing thing was that it wasn't the other way around. When Harry tried to be cheerful for her, it helped.

But where was God? Her God? Harry's God? The God of Abraham? There was no use pretending he wasn't there, a God who is not only there in posies and roses, but in pain. It sounded so awfully false to say that pain was sanctifying and redeeming Harry. It seemed useless. This may be something to say to your own pain, but it sounds like thin gruel when you apply it to others. Besides, Harry didn't need it. He had no urge for forgiveness. He was still trying to find a way to forgive God.

She held his hand as a way out of doubt. It was awful that another person's agony was a way to learn to believe, to believe even in your own moment of doubt. And she was reminded of all the theological questions, but especially the question of evil — of evil, sickness, and death. And of all the great solutions that man had brought to this question, none, positive or negative, seemed to be sufficient. Consider, O Lord, poor Harry. Nor were nihilism, cynicism, skepticism, ungodliness helpful in the face of death — they were only meeting death with death. A good meal? Harry would laugh at that one. He once threatened to write a will that specified a big black hearse full of flowers, and then a banquet — on him — a big meal at his favorite restaurant for all those who said farewell.

But to Rachel the only answer that made any sense was the theology of silence. *And Aaron held his peace.* And so did Job. It was a Jew who wrote on the walls of the Warsaw ghetto: "I believe in the sun, even when it does not shine. I believe in love, even when I cannot feel it. I believe in God, even when I do not see Him." Harry could have been that Jew. She wished for him that as he slipped away in Brigham and Women's, his hand could be writing the same words above the bed.

27   A Momser

When Harry died, Rachel had something new to worry about. Far from reassuring, the talk with Harry had stirred Rachel's fears further, not so much because of her identity but because of that of Jesus. Was she, too, rejected by the rabbis? That was Jewish law. Of course, it had been a shock to learn that she was Rabbi Solovetch's daughter. That should have made her identity problem worse. But somehow it didn't. What worried her more was that Jesus was a momser, a bastard, too.

Rick was the one to ask when they were having coffee together in the Brandeis cafeteria.

"Rick," she said, "Jesus was a momser."

"A bastard?"

"Yes."

"How do you figure that? You mean the old Jewish legend that a Roman legionnaire was his father?"

"No."

"Well, then, what?"

"God was his father."

"Adultery? You mean adultery?" Rick said slightly wide-eyed. "I thought we went over that one."

"Joseph was Mary's wife."

"You do mean adultery, don't you?"

"Yes. God had another man's wife."

Now Rick chuckled.

"But it was before Joseph married her," he said.

"It doesn't matter," Rachel replied. "It was God's child. Joseph married Mary. Jesus was a momser."

"I don't think this is one the theologians have taken seriously," Rick said seriously. "God an adulterer."

"I'm a momser, too," Rachel blurted out. Despite herself, tears began to trickle down her cheeks. She told Rick about Harry in the hospital, and the story.

Rick then surprised Rachel by explaining to her the concept of the Virgin Birth.

"You see, Rachel," said Rick. "I'm a born Christian. I know as a scholar from the Bible that when Mary was espoused to Joseph, before they came together, she was found with child of the Holy Ghost. But this doesn't mean than God physically made love to Mary."

"What does it mean?" Rachel asked, like a good, straight girl. But Rick wasn't telling jokes. The dishes and cups in the kosher cafeteria clattered in the background.

"Well, it says," Rick went on, "that Joseph, being a just man, was going to put her away. By law he couldn't marry her, but he didn't want to make a cruel example of her, either. But then it says an angel of the Lord appeared unto him in a dream. The angel addressed him as the son of David and told him not to worry about taking Mary to wife."

"Why not?" Rachel said. "She was pregnant. She had adulterated herself. It was against the law."

"God breaks the laws," Rick said. "The reason was that what was conceived in her was of the Holy Ghost."

"What does that mean?"

'Well, the line of David was the kingly bloodline of the Jews. This bloodline goes back to Abraham. This is holy blood, the blood of the chosen race. The ancestral preparation of the evolutionary blood took place in David's line. This was to prepare for the Messiah. The Jewish bloodline was the vessel of God."

"So why did God commit adultery?"

"It doesn't mean that," Rick explained patiently. "The Virgin Birth means that Jesus was the first of the race to be born with the capacity for a fully independent, free ego. Free of the old bloodline. It was evolution. He was to be the first conscientiously independent ego, free of the old divinity. He was to be the first really modern man. It meant he was cut off from the old gods. His knowledge was not to be the old atavistic wisdom. He was to experience modern consciousness. The divinity of the individual mind. This was what 'conception' in the Holy Ghost meant. Instead of conception in the bosom of Abraham. Jesus was the new man."

"You explain that awfully well," said Rachel. "Do you believe it?"

Rick looked hurt. "It's one thing to know, another to believe. I revere Jesus, the man. The Sermon on the Mount. But I don't have faith, Rachel. I was born a Christian without it. I have lost Christmas. Jesus may be the first modern man, but what does it mean for me?"

"Why not believe?"

"And you, a Jew, ask me that?" Rick smiled. "I am the keeper of my own sins."

"Guilty as usual," said Rachel.

"The Bible says that he shall save his people from their sins," Rick continued. "That's the irony. Because in the end, Jesus saved the Christians from their sins but not his own people. He failed."

"And you hold failure against him?"

"Sort of," said Rick. "Behold, a virgin shall be with child and shall bring forth a son, and they shall call his name Emmanuel, which, being interpreted, is "God is with us.' But God isn't with us. Look at history. Look at the holocaust. How can God be with us?"

"Maybe because God is a Christian," said Rachel, with her usual insouciance. "Maybe you're really a Jew."

"Ask Lenny, the professor," said Rick, drawing himself up. A certain sadness crept into his eyes.

Rachel looked slyly, even admiringly, at him: "Lenny, the professor of nothing."

Then Rachel suddenly looked serious and tender. "I want to be a Jewish mother and a Christian wife."

"You want to marry Lenny?" said Rick, with a sudden contortion.

"I want a child by you."

"That would be tempting fate," Rick said. "Mary was a Jewish mother and a Christian wife."

"No," retorted Rachel. "Mary was a Christian mother and a Jewish wife."

Rick laughed.

"I don't want him to be the Messiah!" Rachel suddenly shouted.

"Your son?" Rick pondered for a moment. "Don't worry," he said. "Your son will probably be as normal as Harry."

"Poor Harry," said Rachel. "I don't look much like Rabbi Solovetch."

"No," said Rick.

"Even if he does look like a gypsy guitarist."

"Yes," said Rick.

"Do you think I inherited Harry's higher ego?" Rachel asked.

"Well, you certainly didn't inherit the law."

"But freedom leads to the same thing as the law. The cross. Jesus was free. The cross fulfilled the law. The cross also fulfilled Israel…"

Now it was Rick that looked at her with tenderness.

"Rachel," he said, "let me ask you one thing. Wouldn't you be better off *without* the cross?"

Rachel was silent a long time. It was her theology of silence.

It was not that she wanted to be unchurched. It was fate. She would have preferred still to be in the synagogue. Grandpa's. Opa Sam's synagogue. She would have preferred still to be separated from the men and to long and dream of their world. To have an assigned place in the inscrutable, scary, wonderful order of things. Instead, it was as if she were really Rachel and had gone into her father's tent and stolen the images of the gods. No, they were her own now — as much as God ever was.

28   The Black Guitar

It was only after Harry died that Rachel missed her period. At first she thought she had counted wrong. She kept trying to date the last blood from the funeral. The only thing she could focus on was the day Harry went, as if the calendar had stopped and started there. Somewhere, in Harry's grave, she had lost a month of her life, a cycle of the moon, as if the woman in her had been laid to waste. She couldn't remember if it had been three weeks ago or six weeks ago. Harry's loss was like a hole in her womb.

Nothing was further from her mind than having a child. In fact, her concern was the guitar. The day after they buried Harry, she went to her room and communed with it for the longest time. She just sat there with the instrument in her lap, looking at the inlaid round hole. It was made of twenty bands, some as thick as a fingernail. Two were red. Three were blond. The rest were black. She hadn't noticed that the inlay was black until Harry died. The middle band was half an inch wide, with a curling border in black interlaced with a green, intersecting line, and a matrix of dots in red and green that looked either like border flowers or like a little man with head, arms, and feet akimbo, standing sentinel. It said to her, "Harry is gone."

She wondered if she would ever play again. The last look on Harry's face came back to her. It was him, she realized now, that she had always played for — he had been her genie. Although he had given it to her, it had always been his guitar. The music had been his dream. The sound was him. She had only been the fingers.

For whom would she play now? A corpse? The corpse wasn't even her father, now that it was dead, now that just before dying, it had made its stuttering confession — doubly dead, because it was in the grave and because it was not her flesh. She shuddered. Rabbi Solovetch was her father. What did the rabbi have to do with the guitar? Nothing. Harry, who had given her the gift of music, had dispossessed her by dying. Instead of a legacy, he had taken away her heritage. The guitar was meant to be hers. What did she want with a rabbi? The music was Harry's testament. It always had been. That was her inheritance, not Jewishness, not the Halakhah. She felt cheated that Harry, after a lifetime of loving, had left in his will not a guitar, but a new father.

She wondered if she could ever play again. What if the sound came out like Rabbi Solovetch, the guttural, stony voice of a sermon, the sound of the cantor in the synagogue, a Hebrew chant instead of a song. "The song of the piano is a discourse, the song of the cello is an elegy, but the song of a guitar is a song" — Andres Segovia. But what if suddenly the song of her guitar was the gravel voice of Rabbi Solovetch? What if the strings of her guitar, instead of singing a song of things that really are, began to speak commentaries of the law, with Rabbi Solovetch's beard, and his black hat? A black guitar? She had always thought of her guitar as blue, like Rick's eyes.

The silence of the instrument seemed to lie over Harry's grave like a shroud. He hadn't meant to take love away from her by dying, but she lost him, and she lost her ancestry at the same time. Everything that Harry had tried to be — free, liberal, unfettered — her guitar had tried to be. Harry wanted to dance. Her guitar played dances. Harry wanted to be a gypsy. Her guitar was Romany. It was the voice of the wanderer trying to escape the ancient affliction. It was the sound of Pesah when the Jewish people escaped the slavery of the Pharaoh. It was the tinkle of joy when the soul of persecution found freedom from the inner pharaoh, the bondage within themselves. Quixotic, from afar, it was the sound of the individual escaping from the collective guilt. It was Don Quixote humming on his horse as he rode through the landscape of the inquisition tilting at windmills. All those images were the sound of Harry.

Now they were silent. He had only been a foster father, and now he was dead. The ancestral past reasserted itself in the dumpy shape of Rabbi Solovetch. It was as if someone had suddenly spilled old blood on the soundboard. The *Torah*. The *Halakah*. The *Midrash*. The law. The rules. The past had somehow claimed its own, and the wood and strings that had been a magical boat to paradise, a free ride, was now locked in the chains of the generations, the determinism of the law.

She knew now the guitar had been her redeemer. It was a messiah. On it she had worked out the songs, overcoming fate. The scales and dances had been her mode of redemption. Now a new father figure, in a black coat and hat, with a black beard, had stepped across the still life of the guitar, the Picasso picture, the cubistic future, and cast a shadow on the music of affliction, guilt, the temple, slavery, and the law.

At these thoughts, Harry seemed to cry in his grave. Rachel wondered why she had not buried the little Chinese guitar of her youth with Harry so that as a ghost he would have had something to play. Then she realized that she would have to be Harry's ghost. She would have to play a dirge for him.

She raised the instrument and plucked a low E. The guitar seemed to shudder. Then she closed her eyes and launched into Manuel de Falla's homage to Debussy, the dark, brooding piece that was the only guitar music he ever wrote, for her the greatest guitar composition of the century. She let the thick chords wash over her like a funeral march, a black coffin pulled by a donkey. It seemed to her she had never played so well. There was a profundity to the music that she had never heard before. It was not blue; it was black. And when she was finished, she thought not of Harry, but of Rabbi Solovetch. A thrill, a shiver, of a new identity overtook her, as if she were draped in mourning, with a prayer shawl. She wondered if this, this song of a raven, was her new self. It pleased her because it was not a trivial dirge. There was true joy in it, too, like a Jewish folk dance. In a flash she knew that Harry would approve, that maybe even this was why he had told her the truth of her real father.

Her next thought was of Rick. Suddenly she wanted to tell him of her discovery, to play him the Manuel de Falla piece, to tell him that, after all, she was not a washed-out liberal, an armchair progressive, a Jewish-American, but a real Jew, a Hasid, with roots going back four thousand years — that she was Rachel, Jacob's wife, and that she had stolen the images of her father out of his tent but now returned them.

The elation lasted a minute as she got her hat and coat, but then she remembered the Messiah, the Messiah to come, and Jesus, the marginal Jew nailed to the cross in the dust of old Jerusalem, and she was suddenly back in America, in the twentieth century, a girl with a guitar, a girl in search of herself and the future.

Rick was at home in his loft. It was raining, and a jagged cloud hushed the sky. She was wet and bedraggled.

"The girl with the suitcase," she said. She stood in the doorway holding the black guitar case. The brass buckles on the case were all that shone. Her eyes had lost their sparkle, but they glowed blacker than usual.

"You didn't bring your pajamas?" Rick asked.

"You want me in pajamas?"

"You've got your guitar."

"That's all I have," said Rachel as she went in.

Rick rummaged around, eyeing her. "What's wrong?" she asked. "Something has changed."

"Lost a father, that's all."

"Hey!" said Rick. "You've still got his guitar."

"It's not his guitar," Rachel broke down.

Rick turned thoughtful. He had not been close to his father that way. His dad was a distant person, a figure in the world, a voice of counsel, but not a beloved one. There was a Christian coolness about his paterfamilias, as if Joseph knew that he was not the child's father — that God was in heaven. The father was not an earthman, but a guardian. He kept his distance. It had always been that way as long as Rick could remember. In some ways, he had been closer to Harry than his own old man.

"Harry is still Harry," Rick said.

"I'm a momser," Rachel added. "A Jewish bastard. I'm not even a Jew."

"What do you mean, not even a Jew?"

Rachel explained that according to Jewish law a momser was not even a full Jew and that they had no rights as Jews.

"This isn't Israel," Rick suggested.

"Everywhere is Israel," Rachel said. "I'm just a girl with a guitar. I have no race. No religion. No father. No family."

"You have me," Rick offered.

"You're a Christian. What do I want with a Christian?"

"It's better than nothing."

Rachel sat down. "A Christian is worse than nothing. You're a gentile. According to law, I can't even marry you."

"We can live in sin," said Rick. "At least Jews and Christians have sin in common."

Rachel took out her guitar. "I want to play you a piece," she said. "For Harry."

"I'll make coffee," Rick said.

"No. Sit and listen."

Then she played the Manuel de Falla piece again. The same magic happened. The tones flooded out like a black and somber dirge. She touched new depths. Rick sat and listened, growing more and more moved. When she finished, they sat in silence for several moments, heads bowed.

"You've never played like that," Rick said finally.

Rachel answered. "I never felt that way before. It's the rabbi's dirge. Rick, make love to me. I'm afraid I'll lose it all."

He took her in his arms, and they moved behind the partition, where the bed was. He undressed her slowly and she didn't complain. Then he pushed her onto the bed. Rick was like a lion when it came to love, his mane suddenly spread, a look of power overcoming him. He was strong. But his paw was soft as a cat's paw, too.

After a long kiss, Rachel said, "I think the most perfect lover I've ever had is myself."

Rick answered, "Everybody probably can say that."

"It was true, until you, maybe."

"I'm improving."

He leaned on an elbow and bent over her.

"And you?"

Rick said, "Well, it's true. Girls are generally awkward."

"Boys do the wrong thing at the wrong time. They don't know what they're touching. It's because they're not really in you. A girl knows what to do to herself because she knows when she's going to come."

"Girls do the wrong things, too," Rick suggested.

"No. Not a real woman. A real woman knows."

"They're awkward, too. Masturbation is different. You do it right to yourself. Making love should be as good, only you do it to the other. It could be better. Making love to you, for instance, though, is like making love to myself. Only you're more beautiful."

"It's being inside ourselves that counts," Rachel said. "I could tease you to death. Men and women never seem to talk about it — together, I mean. It's in books. People write about it. But they don't talk, not together."

Rick said, "Oh, yeah. It's hush hush. Maybe it doesn't want to be talked about. Maybe that's obscenity. It wants to be done."

"Yes," said Rachel, "but they're things one never quite understands."

"Now you're talking about technique. The best technique is love. If you really love the other body — the other person — everything happens naturally, as if it were a discovery."

Rachel answered, "In theory, yes. But, still, one has to know about the holes and things."

"I suppose you're right," he said, toppling her back on the bed. "And there's air and feathers and whips and chains and God knows what else, but one doesn't need to do everything. Isn't it enough that you're Rachel, and I love you?"

"Maybe."

And they made love. While she lay back under him, she thought of the wreathe on the guitar.

29   The Facts of Life

Afterward, she raised her head.

"Rick, do you think I'll recognize him when he does come?"

"Who?"

"The Messiah."

"Come on, Rachel."

She brooded. "It doesn't matter to you. For you, it's easy. Jesus already came. Christ is money in the bank. It's like a savings account. You already have it. All you have to do is spend it. That's charity. You already have charity because God gave it to you. For a Jew, it's hard. Who knows what will happen?"

"A Christian carries the cross, too," said Rick. "I just wish I could make it easier for you."

"Well," said Rachel, "when the Messiah comes, is he going to be a person or a god?"

"Lord!" said Rick. "The Christians fought that one out the first time. Can't you get your mind off this thing?"

"No," she said. "It's a question of redemption. Who's going to redeem us for what we've done?"

Rick was thoughtful for a moment. "You mean sex?"

It was Rachel who was quiet this time. "No," she said. "Sex is a Christian problem. Augustine made it a sin. Sex isn't a Jewish problem. We don't believe it's dirty."

They both lay looking at the ceiling, as if a hand would write a message there to save them. Then Rachel sprang up and started jumping up and down on the bed.

"Cocks, cunts, fuck," she cried. "Shit, dorks, cocksuckers, motherfuckers, tits, screw, cornhole, bug, piss, buggers, farts, asshole, suck, boobs, prick, blow job!"

She was screaming.

Rick looked alarmed.

"Who thinks of this kind of language?" Rachel shouted. "Why are there no beautiful words for these things?"

She was still jumping up and down on the bed and she began to kick Rick. "Why do people mouth these words all the time, on streets, in schools, in bathrooms, even while they're eating. Answer me! Why have our writers, our famous writers, turned all these words into obscenity and pornography? They've made all love four-letter swearing. Just talking nowadays, you get a bad taste in your mouth. And listening! But these things aren't innately disgusting. They're not necessarily obscene."

"It's their minds," said Rick.

"Blow job. How do you like that one?"

"Uh huh."

"It sounds like lube and oil change. Where do people get this stuff?"

Rachel sat down on the bed. Rick was spent, naked. "I mean, you're not obscene. Some of what lovers do is only obscene if you talk about it. Why it that? I mean, cunnilingus is sort of cute as a term, but a blowjob? What is that? It's a garage. Who wants that? When you're making love, it's natural to kiss. There's no more obscenity in it. It's just the mentality of people who make-up the language who are disgusting."

"It doesn't bother them," said Rick. "They never think about it. There's no connection between their brains and their mouths."

Rachel pouted. She lay back down on her back. "An Italian girl making love looks up at the ceiling and says, 'Mama Mia.' But a Jewish girl looks at the ceiling and says, 'Benny, the ceiling needs paint.'"

Rick chuckled. "So shall I get up and fix the loft?"

"No," Rachel said, pulling him to her. "You're a Christian. Make love to me again!"

When he was spent, and she was still looking up at the ceiling, Rachel said to Rick, "The facts of life were thought up by divinity."

"That's so," he said.

"If a man and a woman make love when the woman is impure, do you think they have impure children?"

"Mongoloids," said Rick.

"Mongoloids aren't impure. They're loving."

"That's why Jews have so few children. They only make love when they're pure," said Rick.

Rachel looked naughty. "What about if you have a foreskin? That's impurity, too. How are the children born then?"

"Blind," said Rick.

"Not if you wash," said Rachel.

They both went into gales of laughter. Faith may lessen the hardships of life, but humor also lessens the hardships of faith.

30   The Rabbi

"I'm going to him," Rachel told Rick.

"What about your mother?"

"She doesn't know."

<u>She doesn't know</u>. To Rick, that seemed to express all the ancient antagonism between mothers and daughters. Rachel had a mother, Deborah, a good mother, yet it was not enough. There was never an attitude of leave things well enough alone in this world, but the daughter would always go ahead of the mother and stir up trouble. Now she would stir up old Rabbi Solovetch.

The synagogue was out on Avenue B in a dour brick community building that had a small cupola for skylights and the rabbi lived next door. Rachel grew solemn as she approached her father's house, suddenly not knowing what his reaction would be to her unexpected appearance. What if she were truly unwanted?

She had not thought of this. She had not thought of the rabbi's position, his legalities, the idea that she might be to him an unpleasant reminder of the past, a source of guilt, an embarrassment. She had not thought of those things in her impetuous quest to solve the riddle of her existence, and she had not let Rick warn her. Nor had she thought of what it might mean to Deborah. She didn't realize it was a kind of selfishness driving her to seek a father, that Harry had been to her all a daughter could want, that in the desert it might be better to leave a stone unturned.

She rang the bell. The sound of it seemed to echo inside.

The rabbi himself answered the door. He peered at the girl standing on his doorstep with the black case of her guitar. The rabbi coughed. "And who is it, if I may ask?"

"Rachel Rosevale."

"Oh. I see," said the rabbi after a moment's pause. "And what is it?"

"I want to see you," said Rachel. "It's important."

The rabbi immediately thought Rachel was pregnant. In trouble. A flood of memories went through his pudgy brow. He remembered when Deborah had come to him more than sixteen years before, also at the synagogue, to tell him she was pregnant — with his child. He remembered his cowardice, how he secretly wondered if it wasn't Harry's or someone else's, how he scrambled to think of some solution. A life is a given. It is a final judgment. It breaks all codes. It demands to be met full on. Yet even his first reaction had been the scalpel. This girl who now stood before him — his first reaction to the thought of her existence had been instantaneous: abortion. It had taken an ethical effort on his part, a pure determination of the will, to overcome his own instinctive reaction to murder the child, to simply remove life in order to simplify it. Deborah, so many years ago, had understood and waited for him to control the shock. It was ironic how fast a baby can end a love affair. He had a wife. He had children. He had the synagogue. It was craziness, the Song of Solomon, that had led him astray, a sort of pride, a vaingloriousness, the temptation of something forbidden. He had always been a conservative boy, and Deborah, when she appeared in the congregation, had been like a Chagall, an image from the twentieth century, an invitation to taste the delights of freedom, pleasure, modernism. He was newly installed and full of a new sense of power and masculinity. She had seemed like a Susannah.

Then he had said to Deborah, "Let it be Harry's child."

Now Rachel said to him, "Can I come it?"

The rabbi led her up the dark hall to the sitting room, and then without irony, turning the light on, he said, almost mechanically, out of habit, "What can I do for you, my daughter."

Rachel looked sharply at him, but all she could see was the passive face of the pudgy rabbi, professionally benign, eyeing her shrewdly from across the room. She had never liked him. She had always been scared of him. He was actually not so much pudgy as swarthy and stocky, and she marveled at how much she herself looked like Harry.

"You look like Harry," said the rabbi.

She could not tell if this was the opening salvo of an argument, or a defense. Then he added, "I'm sorry about Harry."

She opened her guitar case. The sight of the guitar, companion of her solitude, reassured her. "I have something to play for you," she said.

She tuned the guitar, looked at the rabbi, and then started Manuel de Falla's concerto. The dark notes importuned the room and slowly made her argument. As always, she began to read thoughts as she played, and she realized that she was playing to a lawyer. "Rabbi" was the term used originally for the ordained members of the Sanhedrin in Jerusalem. These were the judges who had sat in trial on Jesus Thursday night before his death. There was no way she could prove Solovetch was her father, no legal way, and now, as the dirge for Harry floated up from her fingers, she wondered if it was love or revenge that had brought her here. Or justice. But what was justice? That was a question for a rabbi.

When she finished, the rabbi was silent. She felt uncomfortable but knew now that Solovetch knew why she had come. He knew the story as well as she did, better, and now she knew that he knew. There was nothing to say. This was the man that had given her life. There was a bond greater than love between them, yet nothing to say. She seemed in this room to be in the Old Testament, where Esau begat Edom, where "the children of Arrah were these: Dishon, and Aholibamah the daughter of Arrah. And these are the children of Dishon: Hemdan, and Eshban, and Ithnan, and Chernan. The children of Ezer are these: Bilhan, and Zaavan, and Akan." Who were all these people? Who was she? What were all the generations of generations? What was a Jew?

The rabbi's face was impervious, as if the line of descent had ended, ended with Rachel.

It made her angry that in the fact of her father there was no claim she could re-secure. She remembered how Laban had cheated Jacob, first of Rachel, marrying him to Leah, then of his earnings and his leave. And Jacob had toiled for Laban year after year. Like ancient Rachel, she felt like stealing the old rabbi's icons and sitting on them, excusing herself from not getting up to honor him because she was impure blood. This was what linked her to the rabbi, yet — despite the Old Testament — this was what his silence denied. If you were not connected by the blood, what was the point of being a Jew? And what was recognition? What was it that she wanted from him?

It made her angry with herself not to know what it was that she wanted. She could stand the strain no longer.

"What," she blurted out, "are you going to give me?"

The rabbi looked at her quizzically. The silence was a long one.

"Nothing," he finally said.

For some reason, Rachel thought of Lenny Ratkin, the Professor of Nothing. How his bitter lip would have curled. No, he would have laughed. A rabbi. Not even a blessing.

Rachel looked at the rabbi. Suddenly she could see he was handsome. There was a sureness, a decisiveness, an authority about him that she had never noticed. He was a judge. He had all the distinction, even the perspicacity, of a judge. For a moment Rachel imagined him young. Youth is forgiveness. It was a fleeting instant, and then she gazed at him again and thought of the ancient justice, "An eye for an eye, a tooth for a tooth."

"God has blessed you," the rabbi said. And he smiled. She had never seen him smile.

He got up.

Rachel fumbled with her guitar, putting it back into its case with the bright red lining. The lining seemed to glare in the room. Her instrument. She no longer knew why she had come to the synagogue or what she had expected to find.

"One more thing," the rabbi said, as he led her to the door. "Don't tell Deborah. There is no need for her to know that you know."

So her burden, as she looked a last time at the rabbi, was to be knowledge. The knowledge of who she was not. And it was hers to bear alone.

"Thank you for the music," Rabbi Solovetch said, quietly shutting the door. It closed with a click.

Again Rachel was alone, a girl with a guitar, on the side steps of the synagogue. Harry was dead. Deborah would never know that she knew. It was winter. She was alone, clutching the black case.

31   A Grapefruit

After leaving Solovetch, Rachel went in a daze to the hospital, on her own, thinking life is a drama we recite, to have or not, whether or not we know the script — in fact, we don't know our own roles. We enact the unknown. The drama is the discovery of the action. We receive the lines as if they were on an invisible prompter, messages of light that we see only in confusion. No wonder our lines and gestures seldom coincide, and we utter the foolish things that we wish we never had said, wonder how it is we ever did this, said that.

The modern, huge complex was Brigham and Women's Hospital. In the stillness of doubt, the steady traffic of cars and patients was somehow reassuring, punctuated only by the alarm of an ambulance siren coming in at the emergency drive. That was where Rachel went. She had no doctor she could trust, so she checked in as an ambulatory emergency. She didn't know what else to do.

All her life she had been well, except for the Messiah, the mental anguish when she spoke to Dr. Themagorsky. She had thought of going back to him, but he was a shrink. She was depressed, true. She seemed to herself like a mutant. A mute. The world was stifled. A person who could not sing. It was as if a song could not escape. As if distant drums sounded an approaching tattoo. Not only her spirits but her body was dampened. Something was wrong in her stomach. She felt enveloped in an act of despair. Suddenly she seemed awash in gloom and waves of foreboding broke over her. With Harry's death, the Rabbi Solovetch, and now this, the world seemed turned upside down. She vomited. Last night she had walked and walked. It had already been dark. The only saving grace had been the lights in the night, the twinkling of a thousand stars.

What if she needed an operation? The gowned interns and nurses seemed to walk in another world, an antiseptic reflection of a world to come, where Rachel was a patient in a hall of mirrors. It was no longer her, but her body — something was wrong with her body. Maybe they would take her body away from her. Maybe they would take her fingers away from her hand and she would never be able to play the guitar again.

She waited. They could see she was not injured. No trauma. They were sending her up to the internists for radiology. They would look at her organs, her skeleton, her heart. Maybe it was her heart! Awful. Suddenly she was thinking again of the Messiah. Maybe it had something to do with the coming of the Messiah. Crazy!

She wondered why in America the coming of the Messiah is always associated only with something bad. That Jones man in Venezuela, when all the followers drank cyanide out of paint pails, and all died in the garden, or the insane man from Waco, Texas, who blew himself and his people up in the compound. The newspapers and sensation sheets always called those people messiahs, played the stories up, and always the words "messiah" was associated with something lunatic, lurid, insane, horrible, self-destructive, fanatic, and grisly.

But they were not messiahs. They had nothing to do with the Messiah. They were poor, ignorant, pitiable psychotics, sick people, aberrations. The Messiah was supposed to be something good, someone peaceable, someone bringing love and redemption. Why didn't they think of Eleanor Roosevelt and Mother Teresa?

The end of the world did not mean poison, fire, and explosions, but something good — peace, love, charity, faith, hope. The end of the world meant a finish to sickness, injustice, death, disaster, lawyers, insurance companies, fires, accident, injury — how had the Christians gotten it wrong, why did they always envision the end of the world as brimstone and fire? The end of the world meant the coming of a garden. The Messiah meant grace. It meant heaven. But the preachers and newspapers and magazines had it wrong; they always hailed the fake prophets in pages of apotheosis, and always used the word "Messiah" for some bad man, for something sick. Was it part of anti-Semitism, this lurid image of a false messiah, this bringer of badness, this insanity?

Rachel was supposed to go to Israel. Now this. The trip had already been planned. The concert was scheduled. Yet she was scared. She had somehow gotten the image of a black land, a land of shadows, a land of turmoil, a land of the dead. Where was Israel, the Promised Land — the land of hope? Her dread was negative. She recoiled from the trip, as if she were flying to a land of the tomb. Abraham's tomb. Solomon's tomb. David's tomb. Jesus' tomb.

Perhaps it was the macabre eeriness of the emergency room, the doctors, the lights, the stretchers, the sirens.

She thought of Rick. She hadn't told even him that there was something wrong with her. Rick had hope. That was what she liked about him. He had a cheery soul. There was something optimistic about him. He always seemed to be able to pull a rabbit from a black hat. Hope. There was a virtue. It should have been a Jewish virtue, what with the hope of the Messiah, the hope of redemption. But it wasn't. The Jews inherited suffering, not hope. They were pessimists. Conscience, too, was a Christian thing; instead of conscience, the Jews had guilt. Rick made love with a conscience; Lenny made love with guilt.

That's what it was about hospitals — the future was at stake. No one ever lives in the present in hospitals, but always in the past, and the future. What was her future?

She was in the upstairs waiting room now. The looks of the women were all preoccupied, worried, internalized. Rachel wished she could play her guitar. It was still with her, like a doctor's black bag, between her legs. How those walls, those stations, those instruments, those lights needed music!

"Life is what there is as long as there is life," she said to herself as they called her name.

"How are you?" the nurse said, handing her a gown. "Change into this and just wait for your name."

Wait for your name. Ever since she was a child and had written "Rachel Rosevale, Guitarist" before her first debut, she had been waiting, in a sense, for her name. Yet she had a name. Rachel Rosevale. She was even catching up to her name. Her name had traveled to Boston, to New York, now to Jerusalem.

What did people do who had no names, who were only numbers, only tattoos? And now she waited, in the flimsy open surgical gown, for her name — again, as if for a new fate.

"It's probably nothing at all," the clinician said as she positioned her. Buzz. They took the picture. Another position. Buzz. Another picture. And it was over.

"You can change back to your clothes now."

She waited for the result. She wondered if she would ever have a home. She had never had a house of her own, not even an apartment, and now she might be sick. She might have to cancel her trip to Israel, die at Deborah's, never live with Rick. Rick was awed by her now that she was Rachel Rosevale, the concertist. Yet she still snuck off to the Blue Guitar Cafe. The trio still performed *Socegadamente* and drifted off into the improvisation of the bars, the drums, and the guitar. They were even thinking of cutting an album.

The radiologist was a woman who looked serious as she approached Rachel. She was holding the film and wouldn't meet her gaze. "You have to come back for tests," she told Rachel. "You have a growth about the size of a grapefruit. We will have to determine what it is before proceeding."

That was it.

A growth?

"Is it malignant?" Rachel asked, involuntarily. She couldn't help but think of the Messiah, a malignant growth that had somehow started in her, yet it was foolishness — what did those ideas have to do with her, with each other? The radiologist smiled.

"Don't worry, dear," she said. "We can't tell a thing without further tests."

Rachel had a sudden impulse to tell this woman about the Messiah, to warn her, to get her help in preventing the coming, as if it had something to do with her growth. A tumor.

But she didn't say anything. She went away penitent and feeling guilty. First Harry, then Solovetch, now this. The size of a grapefruit. It was some malignancy that had come to embody . her sins, whatever they may be. Suddenly reality changed and health became a question of life and death, a primary fact, a condition that took the place of Lenny, of Rick, of her thoughts, her hopes, her fears. Life was no longer mental, not made up anymore of music, of the pursuit of love, of whether one was happy. Quality gave way to quantity. There was a big black X-ray now that diagnosed the insides of things. Suddenly the future was a gray picture of trouble. There was a growth, a shadow shape on the bright side of life.

Part Four

Rachel Rosevale's Israel Diary

Pregnant, I am on my strange way to Israel. This is *aliyah*, the pilgrimage — by air. Four thousand years of history accomplished in a few hours. The plane is not one of those jumbos, and we have just stopped at Zurich, Switzerland, a neutral stop in the land where the Zionist congresses used to be held at the end of the nineteenth century, when the Jews slowly began stealing, buying, muscling their way back to Palestine and a certificate became the future to repatriation with a country that didn't exist yet, the country of the future that was rebuilding the past.

Was it a move forwards, with socialism, or was it a step backwards from Anno Domini into the time before Christ? Israel, the land of Abraham; Israel, the earth of Jesus. Israel, the kingdom of David, but also the paradox of Christ. Israel, the modern military state, armed with an air force and nuclear bombs, but also a theocracy. And with Arabs for neighbors.

We move onwards. My seat is 19A. I have a view of Hungary, a rolling green carpet of land to the north, and nearby Yugoslavia, rockier, more brittle — it is not like going somewhere in America, passing Connecticut, New York, New Jersey, and Pennsylvania. There is Cyprus, on our left, with its Mount Olympus and the blue sea, the Mediterranean.

We have to go far away, across exotic lands, east, to get to Israel, and it is like flying through a diary, leafing a travel book, hurtling through a calendar. I am in psychotime, psychospace, eating from my little compartmentalized tray, surveying a cloud from the upper side, strapped in a death chair, thirsty.

They say it is twenty degrees centigrade in Tel Aviv. The eastern rim of the great inner sea crawls along the window pane, and there is Tyre and the city of Haifa and a mottled, chalky land to my east. Is this home? Is this where I come from? Is this where I am to go?

The Rubin Academy in Jerusalem has invited me to play the *Concierto de los Oranjes*, the Concerto of the Oranges, by Rodriguez, in the Henry Crown Hall, with the Jerusalem Symphony Orchestra. Oranges. Somehow it is the right subject. I can picture the oranges of Israel on the hillsides, and now I will see them before I play. Agriculture and art — the alternatives to religion and to fanaticism. That was the way Harry saw it.

My seatmate is asleep, a Rumanian émigré to Jerusalem, a modern woman who came to Israel when she was a child and grew up there. She says religion in Jerusalem has the dark mystique of the Levant — candles, shadows, darkness, which she says is all more appropriate than the cathedrals of light and space of the West. Feeling, emotion, passion, mood, the blood.

"What if the Messiah really comes? Will you crucify him again?" I ask, over the drone of the jets.

"What is it to us?" she says. "If he is not the Messiah, he will not ascend to heaven after they crucify him."

"That's bad," I say.

"It is not something we worry about in Israel. We do not concern ourselves with the Messiah. Survival from day to day is too costly. Living is a full-time business. When the Messiah comes, then all the Christians will become good little Jews, like the rest of us," and she laughs a little, adding, "Now, if you don't mind, I will nap."

Well, I worry about it. Especially now that I am pregnant. Gulp! A baby in this world! Just to risk it! At least I had it out with Lenny before leaving, poor Rick.

I told Lenny about going to the hospital and how they found a grapefruit.

"A grapefruit?" He looked really puzzled. I let him think about it a while.

"It isn't a grapefruit, Lenny. It's a baby."

Lenny laughed. He thought it was funny.

I was not amused. They had made me think it was a tumor. "A baby, Lenny."

He became thoughtful. Then he tried to look helpful and said, "Did you get rid of it?"

"No."

"You mean you're going to have my baby?"

"Yes. I wish it were Rick's."

Lenny was silent. He looked profoundly tired. Then, bitterly, but trying to be light-hearted, he said, "Maybe he can be king of the Jews."

I socked him on the mouth. It was the night before my plane. He was bleeding when I left. I just grabbed my purse and ran. Rick said he would come to Israel. Poor Rick.

I look at the newspapers on the plane, today's edition, the *Maariv* and the *Jerusalem Post*. Mainly I just look at the pictures. There is one of girls in the Israeli army picking oranges that I think would make a fine poster for my concert.

But the news is not good. For Passover they closed the territories, locking out about a hundred thousand workers who usually cross the green line every day for jobs in agriculture and construction. The closure causes economic hardship on both sides, but they say it has cut down on the number of terrorist incidents. Thirty wanted terrorist have just been caught. A network of Palestinian arms suppliers was also exposed.

Even so, two soldiers were injured by stones near Hebron, a molotov was tossed at a patrol car there, and in Ramallah, a Palestinian was shot and wounded by police. An Israeli car was burned in Jerusalem. That was just on one day.

Another paper, for the next day, tells of twenty-seven Palestinians being shot and injured in clashes on the West Bank and Gaza Strip. In the Maghazi refugee camp, there is a wide search for wanted youths with a curfew. Settlers chopped down forty olive trees in Kufr Deik near Nablus. Scores of other trees were uprooted at Deir Estiya.

And so it seems to go every day. Israel soldiers shot dead a shepherd and a thirteen-year-old girl. The number of Palestinians killed by Israelis since the beginning of the Intifada now totals 1,216 — on the other hand, since December, thirty-six Israelis have been knifed or shot to death by the Palestinians.

The plane has started on its approach to Ben Gurion. I am excited to see the Promised Land, but I wonder what ride I am really on. Already I am surprised by the arrogance and boorishness of the Jews. Their manners seem so much "me first," even on the plane: I saw young men bump an old lady out of the way and not even say sorry.

Has it been right to muscle the Palestinians out of the way to set up an old kingdom, and why are we so militant? Yet, even as I ask these questions, my heart already goes out and cries for this country.

*****

After we land, I meet my first friend, at the airport — Yuran, a Russian. He drives a taxi. The first thing I ask him is where he comes from. He is the first Israeli I talk with.

"I am stupid," he says.

I tell him he can't be stupid — he talks Russian, Hebrew, and some English. He drives a cab. He got to Israel.

"No," he says. "I am stupid. Otherwise, I would not be here. No money. All the others here, you see, are Jewish, too. Big brains. Lots of big heads. The trouble with Israel is that there are too many Jews here. A Jew has no chance in this country."

He says he has a wife from France and two children. He is from the Caucuses, has not seen his mother or father in seventeen years. He is working Passover to make an extra twenty shekels.

"There is too much competition for a Jew in Israel," he says. "The climate is too warm. Hot people, hot climate. If I were in New York I wouldn't work on the Jewish holiday. New York Jews are not stupid."

It is late in the afternoon. Out beyond the flat ribbon of land between the airport and the coast, the sun is setting on the Mediterranean. The horizon is dotted with palm trees. Already, in the tight little airport with its signs in English and Hebrew and the uniformed Israeli girls working the custom lines, I feel a connection with its chosen people. All this, the terminal, the space, the air, the night, is Jewish. Hebrew. It is an elite nation.

Ben-Gurion Airport, the highway into Tel Aviv, the maritime landscape, the country, is big — but small. It seems like a state capitol. Phoenix, Arizona, is bigger than Tel Aviv.

The architecture is all rectangular, plaster and stucco housing, simple, Mediterranean, baked in the sun, blotched, helter-skelter, a little on the cheap, but neat, slightly Eastern, slightly exotic. The living seems whitewashed by the paint, the sun, the dryness. The city as it is approached is not steely gray, as in the States; the dirt and dust mingle with the road, and only the hotels down on the beach are high-rise. Even then they look vaguely European, Levantine, slightly improvised, possibly temporary, built on the quick, the cranes of construction pointing all around them into the seatime sky.

This is where the great Mediterranean ends. There is no more, and Asia, the desert, the East, begins. The sun is out there in the long West at the end of this Mare Nostrum, this cradle of civilization. There is nowhere to look but West over the end of the water, yet Israel is all east of here, as if the known world came to an end.

I'm staying on the Hayarqon, a shoreline boulevard, a sort of boardwalk. The big hotels are pavilion style, a sort of lost Miami of the Jews on the blue waters of nowhere.

There is a great bustle in the hotel when I arrive, for it is Pesah. Everyone is starting their celebration. All the rooms are rented out for seders. Family parties are going on above on the first and second floors. The halls are filled with food.

From each room I can hear the sound of ritual and chanting. All the waiters have on white yarmulkes, as if it were a wedding. It is not as luxurious as I expect — there is something third world, something old, something almost impoverished about it all, yet also not.

The people are curiously picturesque. The faces are different, urbane, and yet like a family, too — the language buzzes quickly over the hubbub, guttural but not harsh — resonant, very quick-tempered, decisive, and musical.

My room is quite simple, like a family improvised guest room, a little smelly, cheap, even though this is a four star hotel. It would be a third class room back in Boston, but it is clean enough. This is definitely another culture, though, more homey; it's as if this place were not used to being a professional hotel.

Outside the window is a swimming pool that looks as if it has not been installed and is still being excavated. The basin is painted blue. They seem to be preparing to fill it. A few ragged palm trees surround the site, with its signs of construction, not new, as if they had put the pool in an empty lot.

*****

I am just back from the dining room. It was all taken up by a big party, a seder, with several hundred people at banquet tables in dresses and suits and yarmulkes. Only a side section of the dining room is left for occasional guests, and there is no service.

On the sideboard there are oblong plates of salad and matzah, and bottles of sweet wine. All kosher. The headwaiter says I can have chicken if I want to, but I tell him I just want salad.

It is delicious. I eat three plates full — all produce from Israel, which is big on home-grown garden produce, sliced apple slivers, pineapple, and diced celery in mayonnaise. Salad and matzah — the dried bread of affliction. I ponder this as I eat in the cafeteria-style dining room — food as meaning.

Before coming back to my room, I stop and talk with the dark girl at the desk. She has abundant hair. Everyone in the lobby looks as if they had come from some far off, ancient land — Morocco, Egypt, Syria, Armenia, Poland, Russia. Her name is Irit. It is the name of a flower. We laugh a little.

I ask her about the Messiah, and she says, "The Germans used to say that the one good thing about the Jews was that each one had a different opinion. It was impossible for them to agree on anything. So maybe when the Messiah comes, it will be the same."

****

This morning there is a Passover buffet breakfast. Elira, my waitress, doesn't smile. A table in the middle of the room is festively covered with fish, sour cream, diced salad, plums, apricots, tuna, olives, cucumbers, and tomatoes — all grown in Israel. All kosher. A simple boiled egg, symbol of creation, has not tasted so good in years. Jews even teach the food how to taste. Instruction. Old men who look like they retired at sixty-five from other countries stumble around the room, saying a holiday "Boker tov" to each other - "Good morning" in Hebrew.

At my table the placemat, a paper doily, is in two languages: Ken -yes; malon - hotel; adon - mister; g'vereth - Mrs., Miss; bevakasha - please; todah - thanks; meltzar - waiter; tov -

good; rah - bad; shlichah - excuse me; L'hitraoth - see you again; ma schlom cha - how are you?

It is hard to associate all that is evil with the word "rah," or all our blessing with the syllable "tov." But these people are doing it. It is real for them. Imagine them, not in the Tel Aviv dining room but in the concentration camps in Germany, mumbling to the guards on their way to their deaths, "Shlichah!"

This hotel, on a prime location on the esplanade, is improvised like postwar buildings, as if it had been built in haste. The Jews were obviously torn, as if they had built something permanent quickly while having the feeling that they would not be here for long. It is a bit tacky for a four star place, and slightly shopworn.

Functional and fairly clean, however. In the backyard some empty white plastic chairs stand abandoned in the corner of the wall to catch the sun while the desolate pool is being re-cemented, but I didn't take my bathing suit.

Israel. It is indeed for real. That is the first surprise I get when I arrive. A land for real. Not a dream, not a map, not the idea of Zion — but really here. That is what all the signs in Hebrew seem to say.

******

I'm writing on the bus as it passes through the countryside north of Tel Aviv, the road to Haifa. Mediterranean urbanism. In the hills to the northeast, patches of intense gardening and agriculture. No more signs in English. But also not as many signs — less commercialism, more peace.

Some of this must be what the land was like before the State. It is my first look at the Holy Land, with its fragrance of orange blossoms, Venus bushes, Judas trees, poppies, and mimosa against the grilled earth strewn with limestone croppings and loose stones. Biblical images float across the highway, and oranges are on sale beside the road like jewels.

The muted green of olives dapples the steep hillsides. Towns sprout out of the small mountaintops.

We're approaching S'hfaraam now, where the kibbutz is in the Haifa hills, the orange groves come down to the road, and there are vineyards and beds of tomato and celery. The dry bloom of yellow brown dots the road shoulders, and fields of rape that look like buttercups. The Judas tree is heavy with plum-colored, light purple flowers. The animals are with us, too — goats and sheep.

Ahead of us is the kibbutz.

****

The kibbutz is located on a windy hilltop with new stucco slab, prefabricated houses and narrow, paved walks to and fro with little street lamps. There must be about forty houses in all. The earth is newly churned up by the bulldozer, but the older houses are watering beds of flowers along the concrete walkways.

Children are playing. The playground has its own jungle gym, swings, and seasaws with a small plaque detailing its commemoration, a donation from America. Among the houses wildflowers, rosmarin, sage, and herbs are growing.

My room is seven by nine feet. Two tiny windows look west, to the next hills, several Arab villages, and more settlements. I can hear the muezzin calling from the mosque across the valley when I slide the windows. There is one bare light bulb hanging from the ceiling, light blue walls, pine trim, linolyte tile floor. The bedspread is green. There is a small table for a desk. Two angels are framed on the wall, and there are a few books, a knickknack or two, a tiny vase of a few half-dried field flowers.

After I am in the room awhile, I take one of the books down to skim. It is about Yahweh, god of the Jews, but it is not orthodox. It says that Yahweh was one of the Elohim, one of the seven *exusiai*, who secretly appeared on the *Via Dolorosa* in Jerusalem during Jesus' passion, and that it was actually he who played the role of the old man on the street at the sixth station of the cross who came forward and offered to bear the cross up the hill for Jesus.

All that must be occult wisdom because certainly I was never taught that Yahweh, ancient God of the Jews, stepped out of the cosmos to carry the wood cross for Jesus as he toiled up the hill, but it is a nice story. Who else would the man have been? It is nice to think that the god of the Old Testament shared in Jesus' burden this way. I must remember to tell Judy Kaplan. And Melissa.

This morning I read Ganlil's letter in the newspaper. Everybody is talking about it.

"Dear Son," she writes, "I know that as you patrol the Gaza, your head will be high and your eyes alert (I hope) looking around, and we want to see you back with us for a long, long time. So know that we are with you when behind a door or window the hidden hand moves, the hand of the knife, the Arab hand — and don't hesitate, shoot! Nothing is not a moment too soon against the hidden threat, and don't be bothered by the self-righteous critics and the wooly-headed journalists; when you see that hidden hand move, shoot, and know that we will be with you."

But these are the Palestinians who were here on the land before we came back. They have been removed, can't own their own housing in many cases, don't have their own electricity or schools. Their settlements are all twenty or thirty years behind the times, and I read how even the children are turned back at the public pool when the ticket-taker hears them speaking Arab.

*****

This morning I join a small tour going to Galilee. At the junction of Route 4 with the S'hefarem Road, a blockade of Jewish soldiers in military vehicles stops us. The sun is already shining. The road, with its wayside flowers, looks innocent enough to me, but perhaps not.

"Do you want something?" the soldier with a machine gun asks us.

"We are going to Galilee," the driver of the van answers.

It all sounds so strange. The machine gun looks even stranger.

After that the road goes along a valley, the roadside staked out by fruit vendors, hitchhikers at the bus stops. The villages look parched. Desert evergreen and biblical trees line the fields as we pass under the Horns of Hittim. At last, over the hills, we see a rim of blue water reflecting in a bowl of green, the air suddenly soft, the light filtered with moisture. There it is, the magic Sea of Tiberias, the Lake of Galilee.

Tiberias, the old Roman resort, cascades with the curving road down the hillside to the lake, which is bigger than I expect but smaller than the imagination. The resort has an everyday look, palm tree-lined streets, no high rise, a rectangular look, with strings of new settlement housing rimming the steep slopes.

Instead of Christ walking on the waters, there are Israelis traipsing up and down the streets in shirtsleeves and shorts, and when we reach the water it is placid and softly lapping at the abrupt shores. The grass and shrubbery line the water's edge as if nothing happened here, yet the whole sea is like a mystic watercolor.

At the north end of the waters the van stops at the *Missa Christi*, where we have to buy tickets to see the rock where on the water's edge Jesus, after his death, appeared to the fishermen. A couple of vendors are selling trinkets — shells, pictures, fish knives, and holy water from the Jordan in little test tubes for ten shekels. Some of the trinkets are carved of olive wood, and there are oranges.

In the chapel, where Jesus dined with Peter after the resurrection, where he told the disciples to "cast the net on the right side," German pilgrims are singing. Victoria, a British woman with us, is disgusted. She expects quiet and serenity. She is almost Wordsworthian, and she demands that Israel be like it is in a guide book, where in a field of lilies she can meet the God of her thoughts without the bus, the road, the Jews, and the Germans.

In disgust, she marches out of the chapel. She is over six feet tall, majestic in bearing, and carries a walking stick so she can sit, like Ruskin. She never says sorry and as she stalks out, one of the kibbutz people in our party watches her and says, "There goes the British Empire."

I buy an orange and am finishing this entry by the statue of Emmaus, which is in the same garden, the blind man cured by Jesus. It is curious because apparently, according to the Bible, Jesus, though he was dead and was an apparition, actually physically handled the fish and bread and even ate. So, despite being a ghost, he still had power and force in the physical world.

I like the Germans' singing. In a way, it is amazing that they are here at all, in Israel, still professing their faith, despite what they did. The water shimmers. History seems transparent. Time seems irrelevant. It is quiet again. This is a place of silence.

****

Afterwards at the Sea of Galilee, we go back, chastened, to the van and turn in at the tents of St. Peter's Fish Place, the only roadside commerce I see. Otherwise, there are no advertising signs, only country roads. But all the busses are crowded in the disciple's name, and we order St. Peter's fish, a big bony, grilled perch from the lake, the same as the disciples used to catch two thousand years ago.

There are little dishes of hummus, too, and olives, red cabbage, tomato, marinated mushrooms, creamed barley, and corn chips. This costs almost twenty-five dollars per person, but it is worth it for the simple tables, the blue-trimmed and white pavilion, the yellow tent, the picnic atmosphere, the boats, the shore, the sun, the lapping of the gentle waves of Galilee.

I make friends with the waitress. She looks like a picture postcard of an Israeli girl on a kibbutz, handsome and pretty at the same time. She is very quick and has black hair and black eyes. She has tight jeans on, a silver belt, a white blouse, and she says her name is Fhunni — "Like 'funny,' it sounds like 'funny,'" she laughs.

Somehow I see her as myself, or maybe as I would like to be, scurrying quickly back and forth under the pavilion to the kitchen. There is something half-Jewish, half-Arab about her, like a flower of this Levantine world.

Capernaum lies at the head of the sea, but the first thing we meet is a parking lot with rows of cars and tour busses, like prehistoric reptiles, in the sun. Modernity is the chosen means, even for the faithful. There are no visitors afoot in sack cloth and ashes. Pilgrimage has changed. The long overland route is dead. You no longer sacrifice half a lifetime to travel through strange countries in defile, avoiding bandits and thieves. Devotion is packaged now, ready made.

Capernaum. Peter's house. Remains of a modest archeological dig. A few stone walls. Except for the simplicity there isn't much to see — a few lizards eye us from behind the metal fence, salamanders of the sun, but the rocks of Peter's house look like a small police precinct in a Roman slum, overshadowed by the modern, octagonal glass church, which shows how later times, our times, have sanctified prayer in contemporary institutional structure, as if Peter belonged more to us than to the past.

Yet, without this, there would have been almost nothing. Religion has sacramentalized its origins, and the present edifice is now stronger than its sources. Perhaps imagination is dying. It is no longer an age when a relic of wood can move mountains of faith. We need the latrines, the souvenir stands, the new glass and steel.

More interesting than the octagonal church is a fourth century Roman temple, remains of the Empire that was converted into a synagogue. Why were the Romans, to whom the Israelis were enemies of the Empire, converting temples into synagogues as early as that? Had they already perceived the Christians as a worse enemy than the Jews? I buy a couple of postcards and ask the vendor, who says, "I am a Christian. I don't know. The Jews killed Jesus Christ. Ask that Franciscan father there. He knows."

The wind ruffles the waters. Galilee turns purplish in the late afternoon, stretching away still unspoiled, still a sanctuary from the parched south, as it must have been when the disciples withdrew here to this world, with its hidden banana plantations, olive trees, and perfumed orange groves. A strange sense of timeless isolation dwells over the water, and Victoria, the British Empire, who has an eighty-two-year-old lady in tow, to carry her bags for her, says majestically, gesturing toward heaven, "Think where we are!"

It all seems a long distance from the Messiah, the past one or the one to come, a pastoral idyll far removed from a modern, urban, social gospel, from the streets and industry and endless, aimless poverty of the modern world where Jesus has most of his followers today. The landscape is so beautiful that it seems independent even of the ancient story, Galilee, a tale now shrouded in mist and hills, an ethereal significance of the Christ that no longer seems real, if it ever did: an illusion given by time.

How fragile Christianity seems to me in the land of Israel, in the modern world, this mysterious brotherhood of the Christ, of the cosmic God incarnated in the promised land, in real life. Without the rocks and statues of the Franciscans, without the tiny excavations of the fishermen's houses, there would not be anything.

The reeds on the shore ruffle on. The storks rise on the thermals and flood the sky. The wind piles up waves on the water — but does all that make history, life, real? Was it here that it happened? What really went on? Why was this little inland seashore so terrifyingly significant for mankind? For two millennia.

Or is it all a story lost in the sands of time, something with no more meaning for the future, for the third millennium, and only the bananas, the reeds, the storks, and the oranges live on?

****

Israel, the groundskeeper at the kibbutz, wears a gun. Why?

"Because I was lost once in Jericho, and it was very scary."

We are supposed to drive down the Jordan Valley today, but Israel says, "Better not" or "you'll get a stone on your head in Jericho."

The Jews laugh and talk about Palestinians and the West Bank.

"After all, it is supposed to be part of Israel." Laughter.

"It is very bad now, and getting worse." Smiling.

"Follow the yellow line through Jericho if you want. But be sure to turn right to Jerusalem." Smiling.

"I haven't been to Jerusalem in years." Laughter.

But the West Bank is closed. There has been a security change. Our car is marked. So we take the coastal road via Tel Aviv. Laughter. There we detour for lunch through South Tel Aviv, a ghetto of a miniature Europe. Tatty houses. Stucco and plaster left from before 1948. Jewish troops and a sense of laundry. Traffic jammed on the side streets. Small businesses.

It feels like a garment block of New York turned out to sun. The advertising is in big black Hebraic script. The signs run backwards, as if a clock were going counterclockwise.

Then we are back on the Hayarqon, the hotel and financial zone, out on the Moriah Plaza, with the trinket shops, the *felafel* stands, the esplanade chairs. The sound of beachers bonking balls back and forth on tambourines reaches us from the sand. This is where they hold the great Israeli Air Force Show on Israeli Independence Day, at the end of April. We buy *pitas* stuffed with shavings of barbecued lamb. An orangina. We are in another world from Galilee. Tel Aviv is the Jewish idea of Miami, with a splash of Saint Tropez thrown in.

On to Jerusalem. Route One. This is the cross-country parkway, not a commercial drag — there are no malls, not much advertising, no drive-ins. It is a busy stretch of functional highway, with many exits to the small villages along the way, some of them Arabic.

Lots of trucks and busses, first on the coastal plain, then inland as the scene changes from maritime to the hills of Samaria and Judaea, then to the western suburbs of Jerusalem — all within fifty miles. Two different countries.

Bet Zait is a suburb, which, compared to Tel Aviv, is like the Hollywood Hills — residential, green, designed for terrace and garden living. An artists' colony. Here I visit Ari and Jan, a painter and a dancer.

Ari is showing his large watercolors of Orpheus, of music, of the Soul's Calendar, and his translations — we are suddenly talking of the conscious apperception of thought versus transliteration and thrust of images and maintaining the mantric power of the originals. It is cosmopolitan intellectuality just miles from the capital of the Jewish world, Jerusalem.

When I ask Jan about the Messiah, she tells a story of the Jew whose son married a Christian girl and, troubled, he went to the rabbi.

"My son married a Jewish girl," he says. "What should I do?"

"Don't worry," answers the rabbi. "My son married a black girl from Africa."

"Well, we're both in the same boat," says the first man. "We have to do something."

"I know. We'll ask God," says the rabbi.

So the rabbi explains the situation to God, who listens carefully and thinks for a while.

Then God says, "Well, things aren't so bad. After all, look what happened to my son."

*****

Today we get back to the Mount of the Beatitudes. A round, porticoed Italian church stands on the hillside, amid the fields. Galilee stretches like a blue altar cloth below. The site is like a podium above the sea for the delivery of this sermon of redemption.

Around us the fields are studded with thistle, palms, and wheat. A winding road leads up to the mount in the heat. I am so lulled by the atmosphere that I leave my jacket and purse with my wallet, passport, and money in the unlocked van. Maybe Jesus would have approved, but the whole time we are in the garden reading the Sermon on the Mount, I am worrying that they will be stolen. Then the beatitudes are so powerful that I almost trust and forget.

"Every man has his own reckoning," the den mother at the kibbutz likes to say.

We stop at Nazareth on our way back. It's a bustling commercial town tightly encased in a steep valley. We park at dusk on the main street near a fruit stand. Just down the street on the one side is the Salam, an Arab restaurant; on the other side is the basilica that houses Jesus' carpentry shop.

Moslem food. Meze-hors d'oeuvres, and chicken, kebab, and chicken livers.

Outside the window is a penny arcade where an Arab child is feeding shekels into a grab bag machine with overhead prongs that he is supposed to manipulate to pick up a plastic foam dice for a prize. Nothing could be more futile a few feet from Jesus' carpentry shop, but the child is delighted.

My bill is for seventy-one shekels, but the menu only adds up to sixty-two shekels. I don't bother questioning the waiter. Maybe it is an Arab reckoning. He is adding on a few years to my life. I leave him three or four shekels extra and a few brass coins.

I tell Varda, the den mother, Harry's Jewish passport joke — What is a clever Jew? A Jew who has a passport. — What is a really intelligent Jew? A Jew who carries a passport on him at all times.

Varda is not amused. She is German. She crossed the border into Denmark during World War II. They sent her to France. She waited for work on the train before being shipped to Israel, and arrived by boat in Haifa.

"Humor," she said. "That is the best. Trust, mercy, and forgiveness."

******

Today is Good Friday. At three o'clock in the afternoon we are on Mount Tabor. It is not dark. There is no earthquake. Only an argument with Victoria as to whether the mountain where Jesus appeared before ascending to heaven is small or large, a hill or a mountain.

The curlicue road we are on snakes up from Ibiri, over the valley, southeast of Galilee. Taxis are coming up and down the one-track road, which leads to a three-hundred-sixty-degree view at the top.

The parking lot is packed with crushed white limestone. Under the pines and cedars there are families picnicking, but they look Arabic. Maybe they are poor Christians.

So that is the Mount of the Transfiguration! Children are playing tag among the picnic tables. Clouds are scudding like paintings in the rich blue sky. All around there is a view of maybe a score of towns and settlements — Dubiriya, Ein Bahel, Ein Dor. Mount Tabor, like a giant anthill, or turtleback, is only five hundred sixty-two meters high, but it seems much higher. The sheer surroundings give it a greatly magnified sense of height. Tourists are coming and going, but there is no bus for them to get up and down the mountain.

I think Jesus would have been pleased. A 1944 plaque in the garden commemorates the restoration of the ruins. The new basilica is in old Tuscan style. An American Franciscan brother stands at the door, blocking access since there is a baptism going on.

Several babies are on hand. There is a little plastic tub, yellow and garish in the stone surroundings, for full emersion. The mothers hold the babies up, naked, high over their heads.

The crowd turns west. They rub in the salt and oil. The Franciscan is very stern and authoritarian with the tour guide, who is letting his group in. The Franciscan doesn't want him to disturb the baptism.

In the apse of the church there is a mosaic of Peter, John, James, and the transfigured Jesus.

In the garden, Victoria, with her crisp British accent, tries to tell me of Jesus' last three years when he had been baptized by the spirit of Christ. She says that Galilee, with its ethereal atmosphere, is the scene of the feeding of the five thousand and the transfiguration; Judea, with its hard, dry crystalline desert is the scene of the baptism, the emersion of the physical body; and Golgotha, in Jerusalem, the Mount of Death, is the site of the crucifixion, an experience of the ego, of the total being.

While she is talking, I have a sudden urge to go to the bathroom. I hurry over to the picnic area toilet, where they have a hole in the ground, next to the ashcan and trash area. It is very smelly.

So I peed on the Mount of Beatitudes and shat on the Mount of the Transfiguration. May God forgive me.

That afternoon we drive to Accre past the Arab village of Bu'aina. This is a detour because Victoria says she wants to see a real Arab village. The road is gutted, the children are loose. A mosque hangs on the hillside, the only structure that has a finished look.

The rest of the village is mud gray. Disconsolate Arabs hang behind the doors and windows. There is a feeling of unemployment, of segregation, a backwater ditch, undrained streets.

We are afraid at any moment of running over an Arab child that we can't see, that maybe someone has thrown under our wheels. The road is a dead end. We have to turn. There are no shopfronts.

But suddenly a beautiful fourteen-year-old Arab girl in a white and blue gown is standing there, eyeing our van — a puzzled, cool, hurt look in her eyes. I want to take her home with me, away from here, and be her sister.

But a burly Arab man shouts from the doorway, "What are you doing here? What do you want? Go away!"

The road sweeps down the plains of Haifa. New rectangular apartment houses stud the blocks throughout town.

Then it becomes white. The seashore. Small ocean waves are rolling onto the rocky shelf under monolithic Crusader walls and the old lighthouse. The Arab children are watching the bigger boys play soccer in a courtyard with medieval porticoes. The town is punctured with arches and passageways.

A little Arab boy comes up and gives me high five. Near the restaurant is Joseph and Elia's souvenir shop, with scarves, tiles, vests, figurines, and plates.

Joseph says, "Welcome" in English.

I say, "Shalom."

He is Christian. He says, "Whatever."

"Why are you Christian," I ask Joseph.

He shrugs. "Because of my parents."

Abu Christo's is the best restaurant in town, a fish place. They have twenty kinds of fish. Abu is Arab, Christo is Christian. It is a partnership, with a cement floor, blue tablecloths, trestle tables, wood chairs, and glass lamp fixtures.

Salmir Abu Elias, one of the owners, serves. He is a Christian and smiles with bright teeth at me — a wiry man, dark, dignified. He shows me the crucifix around his neck. He likes to joke. We are celebrating Victoria's birthday, having grouper.

Abu takes me into the kitchen and shows me the basin of fresh fish on ice. He asks me to select our grouper. When it comes on the plate, grilled, it looks very different, like a Flemish still life. The head is large, the gills of death protruding, and the fish head looks like a grotesque. Someone remembers that it is Good Friday and that Jesus' body down from the cross would have looked like this fish.

"We are eating the skull of Golgotha," Victoria says bleakly.

Jacov is with us. He has been in the Israeli army, and there, in the barracks, he read the New Testament for the first time. The one phrase that turned him to Christianity was, "Love your enemy." Not just your neighbor — that was Jewish enough — but your enemy. That really surprised him.

Yosere is also with us, the leader of the kibbutz. He agrees that there is no reason for a Jewish girl to convert; he says converts become the worst fanatics because although they were orthodox before, after converting, nothing has changed except now "they are the only ones." Like St. Paul. A convert to Christianity starts out celebrating the Christian holidays but then as time goes on finds that the Jewish holidays have everything in them anyway.

Yosere says the kibbutz, coming together, is not a spiritual impulse but an economic and social impulse that teaches the community necessity. Being separated from the parents as a child is hard, but it is no longer done, yet it taught them something. "Afternoon with our parents sometimes saved us," Yosere says.

We are talking about the twentieth century and how it started as a new, modern impulse when Victoria suddenly says, "Then American Evil came."

I think of Germany and the rise of Nazism. None of us can understand what Victoria means. Perhaps she is still mourning the British Empire.

Again we go on our way to Jerusalem. This time we stop at Caesarea, old Roman ruins on the coast, north of Tel Aviv, with crusader walls. Just south of the beach is a refinery with a bank stop for oil freighters, and tall smokestacks that look like skyscrapers on the low maritime dunes. In the theater, which seats fifteen thousand and faces west, toward the sea, a rabbi is greeting a bunch of tourists.

"You are Christians?" he asks.

"Yes," they respond. "We are Christians."

"You are baptized?" he asks.

"Yes, we are baptized."

"I am glad you are baptized," says the rabbi. "You needed it."

We reach Bait Zayit, a suburb of Jerusalem, where I am going to stay until my concert.

****

In Bait Zayit, I'm staying in holiday apartments owned by Isaac, formerly a poultry farmer, who transformed his coops into a kind of motel. This morning at four o'clock there are still chickens who wake up and cluck and chatter. Isaac is a terrible boaster and says he got chicks at a quarter pound and in seven-and-a-half weeks brought them to ten pounds. I tell him those were turkeys, and he smiles. He used to have four thousand chickens, but his translation is not good. He teaches me the Hebrew word for sad: azuf.

I tell him I am going to visit the general whose name my mother has given me, and Isaac says, "We have many generals. I am a simple soldier."

To reach the general I take a cab to Tel Aviv, follow the Ayallon, the expressway that cuts through the city, out to Ramat Aviv, in the Uqasit quarter, #29, an Israeli-style ranch house with a white stucco, wet wall. It might have been in California. There is a raised living room, and a patio with a white metal garden table, low, and two chairs.

Solomon is six feet, silver-haired, a square, expressive face, skin full of life lines, slender, erect, in slacks, casually kept, seventy. A deliberate, slow listener, he is careful in gesture and inflection, contained in style.

He wants first to hear of my mother. Then he tells a little about himself — how he was in the Ergun, the Jewish underground, from 1943-49, afterwards in the War of Independence. A young general. Commandant of the Jerusalem Sector in 1948. Friend of Menachem Begin, the now-retired President of Israel. I am impressed but raise an eyebrow. It was Begin who said he would help the Baptists at the Second Coming if the Baptists helped Israel in the U.S. Congress. I have never cared for this joke. I explain why.

The general smiles wanly. He says he was operational in the bombing of the King David Hotel in 1947, perhaps to dim my objections to Begin's views of the Messiah. "That is all many years ago," he says. He is a publisher now. "You know what kind of publishing I do?"

He shows me books from the Jesus Series, two-and-a-half million copies sold. Deluxe, minideluxe, and paperback editions. Eleven languages.

"If I put a camera on my forehead and went to all the places Jesus lived, this is what you would see," he says, holding the book. "This is what Jesus himself would see if he returned today."

I ask him why he did books about Jesus, whom most Jews revile.

He answers, "Propaganda. It is good for Israeli tourism." He smiles. His picture is in the book with Pope Paul VI.

I tell Solomon he is better looking now at seventy than when he was young. This pleases him and his wife. But as to living to an old age, he says, "What for?"

"The pessimist," his wife says.

They have six children between them. The youngest, Ari, runs a skydiving school. We talk about Bu'eina, the Arab village we detoured through, and I describe the fourteen-year-old Arab beauty I saw in blue and white and suggest a story: someone buys her, takes her to New York, educates her, frees her.

"Then," Solomon says, "she dismisses the man because she no longer needs him. That is freedom."

We drink a kinley, a Coca-Cola Company orange drink, and his wife serves a light, fluffy Pesah cake of white cream and walnut.

"You are still young.... You have committed some crime.... You have money?" she asks very matter-of-factly.

I laugh and joke with her, thinking of my concert in Jerusalem, and say — thinking of Galilee — "We are all here to suffer."

"No," she replies. "The Christians are here to suffer. We are here to enjoy."

I invite them to my concert and tell Solomon that I was afraid I might be shot if I visited him.

He grimaces in his terribly quiet, attractive way, cool and warm at the same time, and says, "Give your mother the greeting of old love." His almond eyes light up, and I see why she fell for him.

At the Basel Hotel, on my way back here, I meet Hanushka, who came to Israel from Poland when she was three. She is blonde and pretty, a painter with cracked front teeth, silver blonde hair, half forward in bangs, large ears turned well out, a gray silk chemise blouse with fringed collar, white linen floppy pants, black booty shoes; but she is outspoken about what she calls "the black oil of Judaism" — the Hasidic and ultra-orthodox in black. She calls them the scum of Judaism.

"My reason for converting to Christianity was that there is no evolution in Judaism. They are stuck in time. Bad moral vibes. Look at their eyes staring hard into nothing. It is scary. Awful." She eats her fruit tart and drinks a cappuccino.

"If you find yourself, you find Christ," she says. "No teaching is necessary."

She wants the Jews to free themselves and experience things truly. Not according to law. If they have any common sense, she says, they would understand Christ.

"It is the way forward, the next step in evolution."

This is from a girl who arrived from Lodz in 1949. Speaks Polish, Hebrew, English. She says men and women have difficulties because they are so different, but that "really it could be very simple."

Anyway, she says, she has no time anymore for such things. "I grew up. I knew nothing. I was in a bubble. Israel is like the cactus, its symbol: hard on the outside, sweet inside."

****

Jerusalem. Jerusalem.

I had feared this would be a land of shadows. A land of death. A funeral land where the greatest death and burial of all history took place. The land of the grave. Of Abraham's grave, of Solomon's grave, of David's grave, of Jesus' grave. A cemetery of human promises. Jerusalem, where Jesus died, the most renowned agony of all time, the most searing story of suffering of all history. I dreaded it. A shadow over the land, a body on the crucifix that still cries to the Jews, "Take me down."

Instead, it is a cheering, golden city, bustling and alive. A city where the divine has rooted in history — or has it? Sometimes I fantasize that Jew and Arab can only meet in Christ, but I fear that the Arabs are farther along in recognizing Christ than the Jews and that they will beat us to it. Their Mohammed already recognized Jesus as a great prophet, and Mohammed went to Allah from the Dome of the Rock in Jerusalem, so they have a head start; the Christ will bless the Arabs while the Jews are still waiting for the Messiah and the light of the future will touch the Arab mind while the Jews wither in renunciation. God forbid.

But the great village looks benign. In town we take a taxi to the Western Wall. This is the remains of Solomon's temple, the holiest spot on earth, where pilgrims from all over come to stuff notes, called *kvittlach,* into the crevices of stone, asking the Lord to grant their wishes.

I ask the driver what he would wish and he says, "The good smarts — not to be nervous."

I am eager to see my people at prayer. A guitar player with a Christ-like beard stands singing by the taxi stand, "La la la li lu la, Jerusalem." It is an American model guitar.

Over the wall, which suddenly comes into focus, is the Dome of the Rock, scaffolded, because they are working on it. Religious sites are always scaffolded. Sometimes I wonder why they don't let them go to ruin and build something new.

But there they are, hundreds of wailers at the bottom of the wall, bobbing their heads as they read from the book. The black canopied Torahs are on display. There is a hubbub. Separate sections of the wall are for men and for women.

The women are at the foot of the large stones, seven times their height, facing the wall, their foreheads bowed against the barrier, as if they were eating their prayers. They are like children in a secret garden. Dwarfed by the wall. It is the human gesture against the rock. It is a picture of fate, of man's condition, as if these people are prisoners inside this wall. The men play torn toms.

To enter one has to have cover, a paper hat. To the left there is a gallery underground, where men in black and long wispy beards converse, read, meditate, lament, pray. Some are in prophylactics, symbols of God's obedience, which look like leather chains.

The muffled sound of wailing arises from the stone. Some are ululating against the sky. There are shelves of books. More ululations. Delegations of Jews from around the world are gathered in pockets together. On and on it goes. Hundreds of people mill about — blacks, Armenians, orthodox, Jews — all sorts. It is like the voice of the soul bleating against the stone and rising to God.

I am dazzled and moved. I want to stuff a *kvittlach* in the wall for Harry, and another for Rick. I want to sit there at the foot of the stone and play my guitar. I want to die here and go to heaven.

Instead, we enter the rock, the *bazaar,* the old city, passing the rough young soldiers, who always have their automatic rifles at the ready over the square. Suddenly there are a myriad of shops with *galabedas,* purses, vests, blankets, camel hide, chess sets, inlaid boxes, olive wood figurines — then, beyond, a whole indoor department store with every trifle known to man, spice bags with rosmarin and saffron next to plastic toys and brooms. Here goes on the eternal bargaining over the price of things, the price maybe, of a man's life. In the end it all comes down to how much it is worth, how much we are worth — thirty pieces of silver. Passageway after passageway of medieval shops, where for four thousand years the souls of Jerusalem have walked and bargained in the shadow of divinity. Finally we come to the Damascus Gate on the other side of the old city, and we stop for a coffee at the tiny Cafe Gate.

I can't help thinking of the Arabs in the cafe, the fourteen-year-old girl in Bu'eina, who she is, who she might be. What if someone had given her a guitar when she was a baby — an Arab guitar. Had the Moors played guitars, was the Spanish music part Arabic, part Arabesque? And who had these people worshipped before the sixth century — Allah? Or hadn't Allah been born yet? Abraham threw Hagar with Ishmael out of the house in Egypt, into the desert, and the Arabs were descended from Ishmael — but weren't they all Jews really? Sons of Abraham. And Allah — where had he been at the time of Jesus? What kind of a God is it, created in the sixth century under Mohammed, who is born after creation?

In the souk cafe I can't help thinking how fantastical all this religious fanaticism is when, coming and going, people of all kinds are rubbing shoulders as if there were no guns, no grenades, no hatred, no fear, no bombs, no terrorists.

All life should be a souk — people should be able to find what they want. The future, not the past, should be more important. Maybe that is what the Messiah should be, the future — but wasn't that what Jesus had offered? A future?

It is a short walk outside the walls from the Gate of Damascus to the Garden Tomb, where Victoria wants to go, where some say Jesus was crucified, but it isn't open yet. We pass a police barricade, where two Israeli soldiers are roughly searching a Palestinian whom they have spread-eagled against the wall. He doesn't seem to take it seriously and keeps trying to smoke, but they jerk him back against the wall and give him a body search. He can't get his cigarette lit. He acts as if the soldiers don't matter, yet he himself is helpless.

I sit cross-legged in the alleyway, waiting for the gate to the tomb to open, and a fly buzzes around and lands on my arm. I don't think but raise my other hand like a cobra and strike. My blow cripples a wing. The fly staggers around ludicrously in the sun, trying to fly. It goes into take off, buzzing its one wing, lands screwed up on its back, then rights itself and tries again. Same result. Slowly death approaches. Belly up in the sun it twitches its legs, stops moving, and lies there, motionless and deposed in the sun. I think of Christ. It, a fly. Me, a Jew.

The English brothers condescend to let us into the compound of the Garden Tomb — a walled garden. It is armed by the British, a Society of the Garden of the Tomb, in London. General Gordon, then commander for Jerusalem, lived across the road on the Damascus wall of Jerusalem and used to stare at the hillside here; the caves resemble the eyes and nose of a skull, and he began to explore the place called Golgotha — place of the skull.

John Snooze, a radiologist from England on a three-month volunteer tour of duty, is our guide. He leads us to a tent above a noisy bus station and parking lot filled with busses. Facing us is a lime bluff with caves. Snooze huffs and puffs and then begins by saying Christ died in a bus lot on the crossroads of the Jericho Road and Damascus Gate, an open public space on a busy main thoroughfare, where the rocks look like the face of a skull. Golgotha.

Above it, the Arabs have built themselves a cemetery. This is a surprise to me since I don't know how the Arabs bury their dead. I ask Snooze why the crime of Christ's death was blamed on the Jews. In my naiveté I have always thought it was the Christians who crucified him. It is their religion, after all. He says there was no crime because it was God's foreordained, voluntary death.

"No one killed him. There was no *corpus delicti* because the body was resurrected."

Then he leads us to the tomb of Joseph of Arimathaea in the rock past a giant cistern that proves the place had been an ancient orchard. There is a wooden door in the rock on which it is written in black letters, "He is not here/ For He has risen."

I think about this as I stoop and enter the weeping room facing two graves. It is said that Palestinians used to greet the Crusaders who came thousands of miles to the Holy Land by saying, "He whom you seek is not here." But I think the English sign on Arimathaea's tomb should read, "He is here, for He has risen." So much for logic.

An Englishman and his wife are angry with me for asking Snooze questions. The man keeps wagging a finger at me and saying, "You don't understand. He is not dead. He is risen. He is risen." A large round megalith was rolled in front of the door in the Bible.

I ask Snooze where the rock is. He says sheepishly that it is gone. He doesn't know. They never found it.

In the vault, the tomb, there is a small window for the soul to escape. Why did Jesus use the door? Snooze shows us a tiny insignificant crack in the stone that he says came from an earthquake. Christ was laid out there on Good Friday, wrapped in linen and a hundred pounds of spices. The women were coming back Sunday to finish applying the spices. The stone had been rolled aside and Christ's body was gone. Did the spirit rise or the body?

I tell Snooze that an Austrian philosopher said the spirit rose but that the body itself was swallowed up in an earthquake chasm.

"He is a fool and an idiot," Snooze says. "No. No," cries the other little Englishman. "He is risen. He is risen." Looking around, there certainly are no signs of a major crevice or earthquake cataclysm. Even here we argue.

Nevertheless, I am very thankful to the English for their civility. They have turned the place into a Garden of Respite. It is not cheap, not falsely pious. They are not fighting over turf like the other Christian denominations at the Church of the Holy Sepulchre, where the Catholics and orthodox insist the true cross stood, or like the monks at the Church of the Nativity in Bethlehem, who battle each other at Christmas.

Despite the strength of these Churches, I can't help but think how frail real Christianity is, real brotherhood, how little there is to go on in those last few hours that count for everything in the life of this imagined Jew — Jesus, whose real goal was the reform of Judaism, the redemption of Jews, the renewal of a real conscientious religion based on the life of the modern, human ego, not all the old rules, prohibitions, and sacrifices.

I am even more reminded of life's frailty when in the bookstore, I buy a postcard from Axxi, an Armenian girl whose grandfather has been killed by the Turks in 1915. The image is still with me of the little retired Englishman gesticulating and admonishing, "He is risen. He is risen."

****

Rick is here. Dear Rick.

I meet him at the King David Hotel, the grand King David, and fall into his arms. He has come all this way for the concert, he says, but I know better — he has done it for me. I don't deserve it.

Hand in hand we traipse through the Levantine lobby, the British Empire's idea of what was proper for the Hebrew Kingdom, where Solomon and his friends set the bombs back in 1947, where British soldiers died in a fight over the heritage of a land, the idea of a people, dead, while Solomon still lives, still savors the victories of youth.

Rick and I go out in the sunny afternoon onto the garden veranda with its view of trees, tennis courts, and swimming pool. There we look and look and look at each other. This is us — and yet not us. It is also the Middle East, four thousand years of heritage, and the shadow of Christianity, too.

They serve King David cups, fruit and ice, a parfait with cream, for eight dollars, and there are umbrellas over the tables, tea, and music. The pianist is a dark girl called Idit, and she plays with a flutist, a Bach prelude, the *Passo Doble*, airs, but despite the romance of the afternoon, it is our same old world where Michelle, the waitress, gets the minimum wage and spends half her time looking for another job.

Rick looks deep in my eyes and asks me to marry him.

I laugh. "I told you," I reply, "if you let me have a Jewish wedding, I'll give you a Christian marriage."

Rick wants to know not only if I will marry him, but why.

"Why?" he says. "Why would you marry me?"

I laugh again. "To save a Christian," I say.

"What will we say to the child?" Rick asks, looking puzzled, like a father.

I laugh at this, too. "Rick, what will our children say to us? About us?"

Rick knows. I have told him. He is willing to father Lenny's child as his own. I put my hand on his. "Don't worry. I'll be a Christian wife, but I'll still be a Jewish mother."

Rick has this theory that Christians are bloodless. That Jews are warm. That Christians are cold-blooded and heartless, pale and bleached. That Jews have the "juice" — but I tell him there are black Christians, too. That not all Christianity is pallid. He associates it all with white churches and stern fathers and bleached-out, chalky congregations.

"I'll even fall in the fountain," I say, "and get baptized with my child. After all, a baptismal certificate sometimes saves you from the ovens."

We walk up the David Hamelech Avenue past the Y.M.C.A. and Hebrew Union College to Mamilla Street and into the Jaffa Gate. The old city rises prominently before us. We come, two young lovers, to the Via Dolorosa — the street that Jesus walked, carrying the cross, up the hill on Good Friday two thousand years ago.

There is plenty of bustle on the street and I can't help humming the melody, "Hello, young lovers, wherever you are," for here we were, for better or worse, Rick and I, in the Holy City.

At the first station of the cross I remember telling Lenny, "You want to deny him because he was a <u>God</u>. I want to believe in Jesus' divinity because he was a <u>man</u>. Face it, Lenny, you're old-fashioned. Despite all the allure of liberal modernism, you really bought the old party line of historical relativity, textual criticism, and deconstruction. The nineteenth century debunking. You don't even see a great Jew when they hang one in front of you."

As we walk up the street, with its souvenir shops, its devotional kitsch, its Arabs and Jewish storekeepers, I tell Rick I am thinking how Jesus, as he took those steps, didn't even know he was a Christian because he was the Christ, who was Jewish ... and all of Christianity came afterwards.

"It could be such a neat tradeoff," I tell Rick. "The Christians could recognize that God is Jewish. The Jews could recognize that Jesus is Christ."

"That's not what they're in it for," says Rick. "The orthodox, the conservatives, the reformists, it doesn't matter who, they're in it for the disputes, the buildings, and the money."

'Young lovers, wherever you are" keeps going through my head, over and over.

"This is where Veronica wiped his brow with a cloth," Rick says, pointing to the station.

"And this is where the old man came forward from the crowd and took the cross off Jesus' back and bore it for him," I say, noting the station, wondering if all our lives are divided into stations, like chapters in a novel, and if I could write, what mine would be. The guitar. When Harry gave me the guitar. Visiting my father, Rabbi Solovetch. Grandpa Sam's death. Harry in the hospital. My first concert. Being raped by Professor Lenny Ratkin, professor of nothing. Rick.

"Do you know," I say, "that legend has it the old man was Yahweh himself, the Lord, who disguised himself as an old man to help his son?"

"My father would never do that," says Rick. "He always said your troubles are your own."

"The crucifixion is self-knowledge," I murmur because I am moved by the Via Dolorosa, despite the popularism, the pietism, the souvenirs. At least Christianity has history. It is not just the menacing, foreboding hope of something, the Messiah, to come. And that history has been overcome. The death is behind us. Our own death no longer matters so much.

We come to the Church of the Redeemer, the Church of the Holy Sepulchre, scaffolded and half-hidden at the top of the winding street, and something Jewish in me resists. This is silly, all this to-do for a marginal carpenter, a bad Jew, a nobody.

But I say to myself, *I will believe. In my heart. My head won't always agree. But Jews should remember they wouldn't even have the will to reject Christ unless he had been the Christ. It is the Jewish paradox, to reject Christ. The Jews crucified Jesus because at heart they were Christians. Our guilt is part of the paradigm.*

At the same time, looking at the Church of the Redeemer, an old pile of decaying stones, it is obvious that not all redemption is fulfilled at one time. That would take a second coming.

"*In us*," I suddenly shout at the top of my voice. Rick is taken aback. But he knows me. "Our minds. In our minds. Not in the flesh," I scream at him.

"*Young lovers, wherever you are.*"

Rick does a funny thing. He swoops me up in his arms in front of the church and carries me across the threshold. The monks are startled. He is my husband. I am his wife. It all seems suddenly biblical.

I am reminded, for no reason at all in the semi-dark inside the church, of my last conversation with Judy Kaplan. She asked me if I were really thinking of converting. If I were really scared of another Messiah.

"Terrified" I said. "Oh, I could answer a lot of things. An anchor to windward. The Bible. History. Fear of the Messiah. The need for Redemption. The Sermon on the Mount. But it would all not be enough."

"Than what?" Judy said.

"No reason at all. That's the answer. I won't convert to a church. I'll convert to an idea."

"But that's faith."

"No. No reason is the answer."

"That's absurd."

"Absurd?" I said. "Maybe absurdity is the reason. It's the insubstantiality of an idea. The frailness. Oh, churches may be strong. Like the synagogue. Built on rock. But I'm getting away from that. No, the transparency of it is what moves me. You can't touch it. I am Mary Magdalene. He says to me, *Noli me tangere* — 'Touch me not.' The empty grave. That means something. The empty grave."

"But how can a man be god, and all that Jesus crap?" Judy said.

"Lenny Ratkin told me not to believe in the man. My professor. He said, 'Faith in the teachings of Jesus, but not faith in Jesus.' Lenny is wrong. Teachings change. Jews teach one thing. Protestants teach another. Catholics teach still something else. Instead, I have faith in the man. The risen man. I mean, I can believe in Jesus because he was a Jew. That is existence. He was Jesus Christ. Jesus is the stem, Christ is the flower. They are one rose. Someone snips the stem and takes the flower. That is death. Death is God. The rose lives in water. Galilee is water. That is what the disciples saw. That is what Mary Magdalene saw at the grave. The rose."

Judy was silent. "You've gone beyond me," she said. "What about Judaism? What about Grandpa Sam?"

"Judaism is a black hole," I said, gulping at my nerve. "A black hole in heaven. It's still good for something. In the stars. It also leads to the throne of God. But not to the son. Even Lenny used to say, 'The Jews will know if Jesus was the Messiah when the Messiah comes.' So it's up to us. The decision is existential. Rick taught me that. And it's not faith. It's reason. Jewish reason."

"It's pretty deep stuff," said Judy. "You're not a Jewish American Princess anymore."

I looked at her. I felt a certain pity for her, this girl who was the first to teach me about condoms. She was still the victim of convention, the victim of unfulfilled hope.

"Jesus was the life," I said to her. "Christ is the death. Jesus dies. Christ lives. It's simple."

"Not for me," said Judy. "I have nothing."

"That's it," I said. "Nothing is it. Nothing is really Jesus Christ in disguise."

Judy shrugged.

"You're getting somewhere," I told her, feeling sorry for the puzzlement in her eyes.

Suddenly we embraced. She hugged me. I stroked her hair.

"It may sound postmodern," I said, "but Jesus was the first truly modern man. He lived detached from his own fate. And that was nearly two thousand years ago. He was conscious of his conscience. A man well ahead of his time."

"That's what a lot of Jews think," said Judy, and I thought she was crying, so close to me, yet so far.

"Well, I'm a Jew," I told her, looking in her eyes.

She looked back quizzically, hurt. "I thought you'd become a Christian."

"I'm a Christian Jew," I said proudly. "If you want a reason, Judy," I told her, hugging her again, thinking of the first time I menstruated at her house, "it's spilled blood. The blood. This is my blood."

****

But it is not Judy that I am holding now, but Rick. We are standing in a dim shaft of light on an exposed rock inside the church. This is Golgotha. The rock of the cross. There is a small wooden protective fence, and in the rock, a hole is covered with plate glass. There are no signs of blood.

We were standing on the rock of Salvation, and Rick hugs me tightly, hanging on to me. *"Lovers, wherever you are."* There, on the place of the crucifix, he kisses me violently on the lips. I laugh.

"Yours is the Judas kiss," I say to him, holding my head back. My hair washes over his hands behind my neck. I seem to hear a guitar in the background. I can't recognize the music. "Your kiss betrays the Jew," I tell him.

"Rachel," he objects.

The monks and friars are watching us. The police, too.

"Kiss, kiss, Rick. Betray me. The true Christ is the feminine mystique. Jesus dealt in the eternal feminine, the woman's soul. That is what will save the world."

"To young lovers, wherever you are."

For a moment the church seems filled with the unfinished business of the world — a blues riff. I think of Harry. The guitar. Under the oil lamps in another corner of the stonewalled crypts there is a Greek Orthodox Mass in progress, and I pull Rick toward the chapel. From some other vault the sound of singing echoes. Candlelight plays on the shadows. The small wicks of hundreds of commemorative lights flicker like thoughts in the stony, dim space.

An urge seizes me. I drag Rick forward to the line kneeling in front of the small side chapel, mostly women in black, shawls over their old heads, waiting for the priest. He is about to serve them communion. Rick starts to say something, but I shush him.

It is naughty of me. I am not baptized. I am not confirmed. The only time I have ever confessed is illegally in St. Patrick's Cathedral in New York when I told the priest I was a Jew and that I had kissed a girl. He didn't absolve me. Now I am back, in Jerusalem, in the Church of the Holy Confession, where Jesus himself was crucified, stealing communion. Rick is shocked. He shuffles on his knees beside me.

"God will not mind," I whisper to him.

"What about the priest?" Rick asks.

"It's the honor system," I tell him.

I have no honor. I am a Jew. We survive as best we can. They have persecuted us too long. We are no longer responsible for Jesus' death, I tell myself, but it is hard to believe.

In his robes and surplice the priest approaches, handing out the wafers. I am without shame. Rick and I are living in sin; I am only a Christian in my mind; in my heart I am still a Jew. Will the priest recognize me? Exclude me? Throw me out of the line? Pass me by?

He murmurs above me. "The body of Christ." The blood. I think of the blood, of the blood on my tongue, of the transubstantiation, of eating human flesh. Now I am a cannibal along with the other Christians. I imagine if the wafer breaks in my mouth, that blood will flow out of the corners of my lips, drip all over me. They will see me. They will know I am not a Christian. They will separate me from Rick. They will cast me in the dungeon. The inquisitors will torture me. I will be burned as a witch. On my tongue, the wafer is sweet. It melts.

It is over. I ate the Christ. I will never be the same. The baby within me will be a new child. I have joined the community of man. I am bonded in the flesh and the blood with the people of God. I am no longer fully a Jew.

And it is a crime. I have committed a crime against Abraham, against canon law, against the church — but not against God.

I have partaken.

Rick looks sheepish. I lift him up and kiss him at the railing. He receives my kiss guiltily, as if we should not do this. I hum. "*Hello, young lovers…*"

****

Tonight is my concert. Will it be different now that I have partaken, have eaten of Christ's body, have drunk of his blood? Will the music still come? Or was it the pagan, the heathen in me that played, a forbidden magic?

I won't know until I am on stage tonight, before a thousand Jewish Jerusalemites, playing for their souls. The law will be heavy in the air. Have I broken the law or fulfilled the law? Their applause will decide. I will play for Harry. Perhaps he is the only one who would understand me.

At the Henry Crown Hall, down past the President's Palace, in the posh residential zone, where they are paying sixty shekels a head to hear me, I will no longer have to feel separated, subjugated, different than the rest, and I can feel at once proud and compassionate, for I have braved their taboos, the taboos of the Jews and the taboos of the church, too. Maybe, even though I am a criminal, maybe I am twice elect, once a Jew, once a Christian, and my child will not have to fear and tremble for the Messiah, not have to await the beginning of salvation as a miserable outcast.

I still taste the wafer when I pack the guitar. Now that I have the image of Jesus' death inside me, it is not necessarily a pleasant one. It is not something trite, cute, or sentimental. It is not a balmy, easy image. It is not a bumper sticker that says, "Jesus Saves." No, on the cross, when he bled, it was as if he menstruated for the world — to cleanse and purify it. In the crucifixion, he laid a giant egg. An egg for the future. An egg of creation: a new world. A world to come. A world of peace, of social justice, of equality, of brotherhood and sisterhood, of freedom for all. A world of consciousness. This world is yet remote, a world to come, like the Messiah, a redemption. Yet he was. He did it. It happened. A man. A divinity. like it or not.

And I have eaten him.

The Henry Crown Hall, with its lights dimmed, will seem filled with all the unfinished business of the world — a blues riff. But at least they won't have to crucify him again.

When I pack my guitar, I wrap it in the new silk scarf I bought in the old quarter here in Jerusalem. Time to go. Isaac, the apartment owner, the keeper of the converted chicken roost, will see us off in the taxi.

"Shalom. Shalom," I can hear Isaac saying, the simple soldier. "Keep your head down."

Part Five

Postlude

A narrow road winds out of Jerusalem traffic to the southwest of the city into low hills and narrow valleys past the new and older buildings of recent years. It passes olive groves recently planted and fields lying with the broken limestone of Israel, which grits the dry landscape like white ashes, and approaches the imposing building on the side of the hill. This is the Kiryat Hadassah Hospital, with its giant rounded bay of windows looking north. Flowers abound in spring, and it is a place for Israel's broken bones, for restoration, recovery — a monument to the health of Israel.

At the end, this is where Rachel was confined.

The hospital houses the Chagall synagogue in memory of the tribes of Israel, Jacob, Asher, Joseph — twelve in all, each window a different color, pieces of broken glass fitted together in the way of Chagall, of flying sheep and harps and violins. The windows face north, south, east, and west, and throw a mixed spectrum of light that Rachel loved. In her final hours, this is where she came with Rick and sat long on the plain benches around the Jewish altar, thinking of their new life in Israel.

Here she thought of Harry, the armchair Jew who had been her foster father, who had tried to be an American. Of Deborah, of Grandpa Sam. The land of olives and oranges was far away from the pluralistic, fractured, bubblegum culture of the New World, and her concert had been a success. They called her a female Paganini and wrote articles about her in the newspaper; she went on the radio and had a recording contract in Tel Aviv. Her photo was popular — she <u>looked</u> Jewish. A musical pinup. And she and Rick planned to open a Blue Guitar Cafe outside Jerusalem, with their old trio.

She wished she could play in the Chagall synagogue, but she had to be careful, to move very little. The synagogue was her home in the hospital, a respite of art. She and Rick sat there holding hands for hours. In the yellow window on the east, too, there was a story, because during the 1967 war, shooting reached the walls of the hospital and a bullet pierced the yellow window. When Chagall had the window restored in Paris and replaced after the war, he left the bullet as a reminder in place, patched, a memory of war. A glass wound.

Rachel used to gaze at it as if at some kind of omen, and once she said to Rick, "It was meant for me."

She died that summer at 2:31 in the morning at the Hadassah. At first they feared the baby would be stillborn, but Funni — Rick nicknamed her Funni because she had such an amusing, unusual face, and smiled from the instant she was born — survived. They took her out at the last minute. Rick was at Rachel's bedside when she died, and she seemed to be almost dreaming after the long, unsuccessful labor. Nobody said she would die, but everyone knew she was sick. Rick was holding her hand when her eyes opened for the last time, and she seemed to want suddenly to shout at him, as she sometimes used to, unexpectedly, but all she could do was hoarsely gasp, "The bullet, Rick. The bullet." Then she died.

Rick was crazed with grief. Every night he watched a late show of his own: Rachel's life. Every story needs a crime, he knew, and every crime needs a corpse — a *corpus delicti*. History is always the same. It is recorded by deaths. Jesus, Rachel had taught him, is the *corpus delicti* of history — but what was the crime? His body, risen, was gone. Without a body, history cannot prove the crime. The charges vanish. Rick inherited Rachel's body. He married a corpse. But her life was a mystery, too — a mystery without detectives, cops, police, guns. Only the bullet. Somehow she had bitten the bullet that was in the yellow window. The crime? Her questions. The body? The body to come, that she so feared, of the Messiah.

Rachel. Daughter not of Laban, people of the East, but of Rabbi Solovetch, who disowned her before she was born, of Harry, the armchair Jew from Brookline, U.S.A. Rachel was beautiful and well-favored, Jacob's niece, but she had no elder sister named Leah. Rachel was loved, but not barren. She did not have to say to her sister, "Give me children or else I will die." Like her namesake, Rachel stole the images that were her father's and used them for herself. She was blessed with a guitar. She was blessed with Rick. She was blessed with a baby she never saw.

It was a girl. Funni was her name. As with all mothers and daughters, they see differently. Rick moved back to the kibbutz and the little girl grew. She wanted to be a good girl. In her playgroup, out by the swings that the Americans had given, she had no Melissa that gave her a cross. Instead, she learned that the Messiah was good, that the Messiah would come and save the world. Rachel had always feared the Messiah. She had an irrational fear that they, whoever they were, would crucify the Messiah if he came. For her the promise of the world was in the guitar, not in a savior.

But in Funni's playgroup, it was different. She heard all about the Messiah. The promise. And one day, just as Rachel had gotten a cross from Melissa, Funni got a golden star of David from one of the other girls. They said it was the sign of the Messiah. But Funni despite everything her mother had been through, despite her mother's long search, said to herself as she put on the star of David, "I am the Messiah."

Rachel was dead. There was nothing Rachel could explain to her. Rachel could not describe to her the Passion and the Agony. She could not tell Funni about Jesus, explain to her that Christ had saved the world, that Funni did not need to be the Messiah. No, Funni decided all on her own that she was it.

Who knows? Maybe she was. Or maybe she was one of many little messiahs born at this time. Contrary to the newspapers, to what Americans think, to the Joneses and the madmen of Waco, Texas, the Messiah is supposed to be something good. What with poverty, injustice, the inequity of wealth, hunger, illiteracy, overpopulation, war in Mozambique, Somalia, Angola, Palestine, Armenia, Kurdistan, Central America, Afghanistan, Iraq — and cancer, heart disease, multiple sclerosis, AIDS — God knows the world could use a Messiah.

"The future is closer than you think," Rachel had told Rick before dying. It was a strange thing to say.

So Funni decided to be it. She kept the secret to herself. She never told anyone, not even her father.

But, in his heart, on the kibbutz, Rick pondered these things. And he pondered the sayings of his daughter, who was a strange, silent child. Another momser.

If Funni was right, it meant Redemption had begun. Certainly, it was about time. The Messiah — a she. Not a bad thing, either. If women can belong in the army in Israel and fly combat missions in the United States, certainly they have a right to be the Messiah. After all, taking life is no greater than giving life.

An unknown Messiah. A Messiah called Funni. The irony is that the Jews, after two thousand years of ignoring Jesus Christ, should again not know that the Messiah had come. A she. She is living in their midst. Perhaps ignorance is bliss. Perhaps hope is better than what would happen if they knew. It is not hard to imagine the motorcade that would accompany the Messiah, the hoopla, the number of motorcycle cops, the guns, the tanks, the military and security that would accompany Funni. Is that what the world needs? Think of the inevitable bullet that would find its way into Funni's brain, if the world knew, from some depository, from some hillside, from some suicide bomber.

Perhaps it is better that Funni kept the secret to herself, that the Messiah is incognito, unknown, unrecognized. Of course, it is a sad commentary that humanity does not have the relief of knowing that the moment has come, that redemption has begun, that the world will be getting better. It would be a balm.

But the Lord works in mysterious ways. It is said that God Himself has been in exile until the Messiah comes. Now she is here. Funni.

So there is part of the heart that says yes to the Jews, Go build the Third Temple now, the time is here, the Messiah is an unknown girl living on a kibbutz in northern Israel. But then they would look for her. Everything in Rachel's nightmares would happen. Funni's coming would be another tragedy in human history.

So, in fact, it may be better that she lives unknown, that even Rick does not know, and that redemption becomes, as Harry hoped, an event of the collective consciousness, a community salvation, in which not a physical incarnation, not a glorified person, not a king captures the mind of the populace, but the act of salvation, unknown, itself. An idea. As Harry would have said, the Messiah is really the idea of everyman himself or herself saving the world. If this were true, then Funni would be the Second Coming; Jewish redemption and the coming of Christ again "in the clouds" would be the same thing. This might save a lot of agony for everybody, Christian and Jew alike, and what would it matter to God if he was really in person a little girl from the Diaspora, unknown, un-hailed? The Divine does not need the world's fame. This event does not need to go into the sensation papers, the radio, the T.V. It might be better if every man, woman, and child, like Funni, had the feeling in themselves, "I ought to be a Messiah." Perhaps if people wanted to save the world, things might change for the better.

To have lived is something. To live is something. Jesus lived. Funni lives. Perhaps crucifixion and anonymity are God's ways.

"The future is closer than you think," Rachel had told Rick. And he remembered it.

Rick continued to live on the kibbutz, with Funni, who became a field worker and harvested barley, beans, and oats.

Existence is something. She was a young woman who knew who she was, but told no one. Her life was simple and silent. All through the years she kept her secret, with the rising and setting of the sun, the flowery spring, the burnt summer. She seemed to live with the land and the universe. Many people thought her strange. Israel, a Jewish state, the new custodian of Christianity, also became the homeland of Funni.

Once a year, on Rachel's birthday, Rick would wander out alone on the hilltop and sit under the Judas tree, with its purple flowers, where he wept.

He also gave Rachel's guitar to Funni, but the girl had no talent for the classics. Her gift lay elsewhere. The gift of existence. But she learned to strum and sing the old Irving Berlin song, the Jewish composer's *God Bless America*. Rick would sometimes hear her at it in the biblical sunset and think of the Promised Land. It made him dream of a blue boat going to the new world.

A blue boat and a blue guitar, reminding him of Rachel, of Rachel playing a song of things that really are.

~ The End ~

Printed in the United States
20750LVS00001B/76-96